John Joseph Hogan

On the Mission in Missouri

1857-1868

John Joseph Hogan

On the Mission in Missouri
1857-1868

ISBN/EAN: 9783743331747

Manufactured in Europe, USA, Canada, Australia, Japa

Cover: Foto ©ninafisch / pixelio.de

Manufactured and distributed by brebook publishing software
(www.brebook.com)

John Joseph Hogan

On the Mission in Missouri

ON THE MISSION IN MISSOURI.

CHAPTER I.

MISSIONARY OPPORTUNITY.

IN June, 1857, the Most Reverend Peter Richard Kenrick, Archbishop of St. Louis, yielding to my repeated request to be relieved from city parochial duty, accepted my resignation of St. Michael's parish in St. Louis, and appointed thereto the Very Reverend Patrick A. Feehan, late president of the Theological Seminary at Carondelet and at present Archbishop of Chicago. This gave me what I was looking for—an opportunity to go into the interior of North Missouri where there was no priest, and there build a chapel or two as nucleuses of congregations. My purpose proposed to His Grace the Archbishop of St. Louis, received his sanction so far as that I was at liberty to go into the country and see it first.

OUTWARD BOUND.

I turned my face towards North Missouri. The North Missouri Railroad was then open for passenger business to Warrenton. West of Warrenton many men were at work, levelling hills, filling hollows, building culverts, erecting bridges. It was a busy scene. Along the line, work was hotly plied. I approached one of the contractors with whom I was acquainted, and asked him to lend me a horse to ride on my intended journey, the purpose of which I explained to him. He replied, "Reverend Father, the horses I have are these you see. They are cart horses, not good to ride. But if you accept one, you are welcome and you can have your choice. The bridle and saddle I have are worn and soiled, jogtrotting here about. They are the best I can offer you, and you may take them with pleasure."

MOUNTED.

I was soon mounted. With a blessing and grateful good-bye to my benefactor the contractor, I set out, keeping the main road that led to the prairies of North Missouri. The weather was hot, being then the last days of July. I passed through Montgomery, Audrain and Randolph counties. From Allen in Randolph county, where on the fourth of August, I instructed and baptized two grown persons, I proceeded northward into Macon county and thence westward towards Chariton river. As I was crossing the Chariton swamp—a wide stretch of alluvial lands on the confines of Macon and Linn counties, I was over-taken by a well dressed young man, mounted on an elegant horse in bright new trappings.

Checking the speed of his steed, he saluted me, inquired my name, where I was from, and on what purpose journeying. I gave him my name and told him I was a Catholic priest seeking a location for a church in these parts. He said, "there are no Catholics here, what then is the use for a church?" Seeing he was prejudiced and displeased with my purpose, I replied, "True, sir, there are no Catholics here now, but they will be here before long, and you and I may live to see the day when there will be a Catholic church on every hill around here." "Yes," said he, "when the Chariton goes up stream, good-bye;" spurring his horse, he rode quickly ahead. Having crossed the Chariton swamp and gained the high lands on the west side I allowed my horse to graze along the road whilst I recited the divine office. Afterwards I rode on some miles and towards evening stopped for the night at a farm house on the stage road leading towards Linneus.

MULHOLLANDISTS AND MURPHYITES.

Hearing of a disturbance going on a few miles distant, on the line of the Hannibal and St. Joseph Railroad, I determined to go there. I found contractor Mulholland with about a hundred men encamped on the hills on the east side of the Muscle Fork of Chariton river. On the hills on the west side of the same stream, contractor Murphy was similarly encamped with fully as many men. Both camps had sentinels posted along their fronts. To the right and left of the camps were the shanties of the warriors in which their wives and children were crouching in terror. Surveying the situation, I resolved to enter one camp first and then another, and by passing from camp to camp to bring both parties to terms; my ultimatum being that they should stop drinking and retire in peace to their homes. Before long, all were at home or at their work again. I stayed there some days cementing anew the friendship that was disrupted but for the moment, and that, as I afterwards learned, continued firm and lasting.

CAMP GARRYOWEN.

Resuming my journey I rode through the counties of Linn and Livingston, not following any particular road and crossing the rivers where I found them fordable. On the evening of August 11th I dismounted at the door of the little hotel at Utica in Livingston county, where I stayed for the night, having seen that my horse was properly stabled and fed. Next morning, as my horse was tired though by no means jaded, I left him in the stable to rest and hired a fresh horse on which I rode that day still further westward into the high open prairies of Caldwell county, which I made the turning point of my journey. Returning eastward I stopped for the night near where Breckenridge now is, at a place then called Garryowen—the camp of Griffin and Shea—railroad contractors from Madison, Indiana, who with a band of good sober men were at work on the grade of the Hannibal and St. Joseph Railroad. There, on the evening of August 12th, I baptized two children of the pious edifying railroad community. Garryowen and Billy Griffin had so many attractions for me, and were so intimately associated, in name at least, with places and persons dear to me since childhood, that I stayed there, though aside from the purpose of my journey, a day and night longer. Early in the morning, Friday August 14th, the vigil of the Feast of the Assumption, I set out from Garryowen for Utica, where having dismissed the hired horse and taken my own again into service, I rode forty-five miles without rest or refreshment; the whole distance travelled that sultry day on horseback, by way of Utica, the Blue Mounds and Compton's ferry, from Breckenridge to Brunswick, being fifty-five miles.

PACKET SPREAD EAGLE.

Arriving at Brunswick, I heard the whistle of a steamboat descending the river, making signals for landing. It was the packet Spread Eagle, Captain La Barge, bound for St. Louis, with a miscellaneous cargo of Upper Missouri Staples; hemp, tobacco, flour, pork, cattle, mules, horses, darkies. My destination was Boonville, from Brunswick eighty miles down stream, where there was a Catholic Church, the only one within the region of my journey so far through North Missouri, and whither I was hastening, to say

Mass on the following day, the Feast of the Assumption. The night was very hot. Mosquitoes buzzed around in swarms, and were unrelenting in their attacks, so that sleep was impossible. Landing after landing was made in good time. New Frankfort, Glasgow, Arrow Rock, were called in succession, and arrivals and departures made without delay, the river being then at high water, but not over its banks.

SLAVERY IN MISSOURI.

The darkies of whom there were about fifty on board, all athletic men, suffered many cruel hardships. Their keepers, a few armed men, held them chained together in squads, so as to hinder them from getting away at landing places. At night, formed into line, shoulder to shoulder, their faces turned one way, manacled with iron hand-cuffs man to man, they were made to lie down on their backs, on the boiler deck of the boat, without pillow, mattress, or covering—a position they could not change for one instant during the whole night, not even so much as to lie on one side. The groans of the poor fellows, as they clanked their manacled hands against the deck, or dragged and slashed in pain their booted heels on the rough boards on which they lay, were truly heart-rending. They were accused of no crime, were torn away without a minute's notice from their homes, husbands separated from wives and children, sons separated from parents, brothers and sisters. All were forced to leave dear friends and loved scenes behind them.   Love of money caused it all.   Traders had bought them and were taking them to trade them again, and for a much higher price, in the slave marts of St. Louis and New Orleans.   Seven years before, when a student of the Theological Seminary of St. Louis, the task was given me to write an essay on liberty, which, like all such essays, was to be read and criticised before the rhetoric class.   My subject led me to make some comments on negro slavery, and somewhat in the strain of Thomas Moore and Daniel O'Connell on the same subject.   "Young man," said the Professor to me, "I have nothing to say to you on the merit of your essay, but this: when you go on the mission, if you give expression to sentiments such as these, you will be driven from home decorated with a coat of tar and feathers, and fortunate you will be, if nothing worse befall you."

SLAVERY'S BETTER SIDE.

But slavery had a better side.   The poor negroes had many virtues, and a gentleness of character altogether their own.   Never, in my acquaintance with them, were they disrespectful or offensive to me, or to any one else so far as I could see.   When on the mission at Old Mines, in Washington county, in 1852 and 1853, I taught a class of about forty negroes their catechism, day after day for several months, preparing them for First Communion, their progress being quite satisfactory and their behavior a pleasure to me.   The negro Catholics of that congregation,

and they were many, were devoted to the Church.
The young men and young women, though not able
to read or write, being debarred from such knowledge
by statute, had nevertheless learned by heart the
Gloria and Credo of the Mass, and several Psalms
and Hymns which they heard in the church, and which
they took delight in singing as they followed the plough
in the fields, or enjoyed the pleasures of home by their
humble firesides. Their masters did not engage in
the business of buying and selling slaves, hiring them
out for payment, or separating wife from husband or
parents from children. They employed them on the
farm to make a support for themselves and for those
under whose care they were, and to whom they were
oftener a burthen than a benefit. The black and
white families went to the same church together.
They lived in friendship and in neighborship, mutual-
ly aiding and depending on each other. The same
parish priest ministered to their spiritual wants. The
same family physician attended them in their ail-
ments. They lived for each other, died near each other, and were buried near each other. The "Massa
and Missus" and faithful servants, choosing in
death as in life not to be separated. Surely before
the Holy Altar of the one God, Master of all, and
under the sacred influence of humanity divinely re-
deemed, there was and could be neither "bond nor
free." The Church knew how to heal the bruises of
the slave and to soften the severity of the master,

and had her influence been allowed to prevail, it would have saved us from a calamity now and forever to be deplored, and which neither blood nor tears can ever erase from the pages of our history. Like Rachel, the Church has ever to mourn and without consolation her children's misfortunes, usually none other than the dire results of selfish greed and atrocious political strife.

HIBERNIANS AND JAEGERS.

Arrived at Boonville during the night, I went early in the morning to the church, expecting to find the pastor–the Rev. Father Hilner, and with his permission to have the consolation of celebrating Mass. But Father Hilner was away on some distant mission and had taken with him the only chalice and vestments that the poor little church possessed. Having heard Mass in spirit before the lonely little altar, I was leaving the church when some one informed me that many people of the place had left there very early in the morning, headed by a military company with muskets and cannon, marching for Otterville thirty miles distant, to quell a riot which had arisen between some railroad men at that place. The painful news considered, I thought it my duty to go to Otterville without delay. Leaving my horse in the livery barn to rest, I hired a fresh one that was soon harnessed to a good buggy; and once again going, it being now about mid-day, I passed over the distance in five hours; happily to find Otterville in peace and

that there had been no riot at all, or at most only a
noisy scuffle between some few who had been drinking.   The Jaegers from Boonville had got in ahead
of me, and having formed line of battle charged on
the Irish camp, which was down in the woods by
the banks of the Lamine river.   The Irishmen not
dreaming of such an attack, and not knowing what
it was all about, took to their heels, the Jaegers after
them.   Soon two men who had thrown away their
hats and coats in the flight were overtaken.   These
had not been in the melee at all, but were nevertheless corralled.   Over them volley after volley of cannon
and musketry was fired amid shouts of triumph.   It
was a great victory for the Jaegers. And to celebrate
it, they soon fell to drinking.   Kegs of beer that
had been emptied, rolled about over the green, and
had the Hibernians had a sagacious leader, they could
have faced about and captured their captors.   Laugh-
ing heartily at the ludicrous adventure, yet much displeased with myself for having travelled so far to see
it, I set about getting supper for myself and horse,
after which, I was soon again on the road for Boonville where I arrived about midnight.   Not willing
to entrust the care of the horse that I had found to
be a good one, to the care of even his owner who
might possibly overfeed him, I remained two hours with
him acting hostler myself.   Next morning returning
to the stable, I was quite pleased to find the horse
well and seemingly fresh for another war adventure.

Of his owner I inquired how much I owed him,
"Three dollars," he replied. "It is cheap," said I,
here are six dollars for you. You own a good horse,
and he has earned his wages well."

HOMEWARD BOUND.

Spending a lonesome Sunday in Boonville without
possibility of celebrating or hearing Mass, I watched
continually for a down-river boat, which came along
at last during the night. Embarking with my horse,
I was once more afloat on the rushing waters of the
Muddy Missouri, heading for St. Louis, homeward
bound. Next day we touched at Jefferson City and
many other places, taking and putting off freight
and passengers. Towards evening we made landing
at Herman. Afterwards, off the opposite shore, the
boat whistled, rounded to, and ran out its gangways.
I was landed with my horse above the head of Loutre
Island. From there I travelled, in the early hours of
the night, sixteen miles north-eastward, arriving at
Warrenton too late to call on my benefactor. Next
morning, however, I called on him, and found him
as I was myself, quite well, and in a smiling mood.
I was glad to return his horse to him, and he was
equally glad to find him lively and in good condition.
Having given from my heart and in God's name a
blessing to my benefactor, which he humbly asked
and would accept nothing else from me, I set out for
St. Louis, losing no time on arriving there to present myself before His Grace the Archbishop.

Favored with an audience, I related to His Grace
what I had seen. That North Missouri was a beautiful country, but a land unknown to the Church.
And that if he would give me his permission and
blessing, I would with God's help attempt to make a
beginning there that might grow in the course of
time. I ventured to tell him, that as Captain Mc-
Clure had then recently found a North-west passage
from the Atlantic to the Arctic ocean, so a North-
west passage for the Church by a line of missions
bordering on each other from St. Louis to Omaha,
should not seem difficult to a missionary willing to
make the effort. Two days later, His Grace called
on me, at St. Michael's church, my former home,
where I was staying for the time being. "I would
not think," he said, "of sending you out to North
Missouri, on that mission. But since you are willing
to undertake it, you may do so in God's name. I
give you these light missionary vestments, with port-
able chalice and altar-stone. They are from my own
private chapel. I hope you will succeed in your undertaking. But if you ever wish to return to the
city I will give you your parish back, or one as good
in place of it." Having warmly thanked His Grace,
I reverently knelt to receive his blessing, and immediately withdrew from the audience chamber.

CHAPTER II

A DUTY SANCTIONED.

THE work to be done, the nature of which my recent journey gave me some knowledge of, and the responsibility for it, since I had undertaken it and solicited for it the sanction of the Ordinary of the diocese, made me apprehensive I should fail. To withdraw was too late. To go on was a duty sanctioned. Failure, if it should follow, I could bear, the cause being a good one. Above all I needed the Divine assistance. This I humbly invoked by a short retreat. Appointing the 8th of September for the initial date of my enterprise, I entrusted it and myself to the patronage of the Mother of God, whose Nativity was ever the harbinger of blessings to come.

FRIENDSHIP'S PLEADING.

But there were difficulties yet in the way. They came from dear friends who regarded the undertaking as visionary. A devoted priest, a particular friend of mine, insisted on holding out against me to the last. Shouldering me back at every street corner on the way to the railroad depot, he almost violently resisted me getting on the cars. I got aboard the train however, and was soon on my way from the

Fourteenth Street depot in St. Louis to Jefferson City, the western terminus at that time of the Missouri Pacific Railway. From Jefferson City I went by steamboat to Brunswick. And from Brunswick by a hired stage to Center Point, a new town on paper, in Linn county, on the east fork of the Yellow Creek, confidently supposed, on account of its central location, to become the great central town of Northwest Missouri, on the railway then building from Hannibal to St. Joseph.

HUMORS OF CENTER POINT.

Besides what was on paper, the town of Center Point had actually one house on the ground—a one story two-room shed, sides, floor and roof of cottonwood rough boards, but without plastering or weather-boarding, and used for a store. The merchant proprietor, whose stock in trade consisted of a few boxes of boots and shoes, and some bundles of ready made clothing, had failed in business, not having had customers. Under the influence of the speculative fever that gave the place a name, I rented the wooden shed from the man who had come to be a failure. One of the rooms I converted into a chapel, the other into a study. Board I engaged at a neighboring farm house. My congregation consisted of a few railroad laborers living in shanties near by. On Sunday I had a crowd from the back-woods to see the priest.

A TELLING SERMON.

My sermon had the happy effect of procuring for

me an invitation from one of my hearers, but of a different faith from mine, and for supper as I understood him. I accepted the invitation with pleasure, and in due time as the evening came on apace, I found my way following the directions given me to reach his house. Soon I was hospitably treated to a plentiful supply of squashes and watermelons, spread out on the puncheon floor of the log mansion of my host, who did the honors of the occasion, by cleaving the huge vegetables before us into lumps and slices with a piece of a scythe, the heel of which, straightened, had been set into a stout wooden handle. If there were any dishes or knives or forks in the mansion, they were not called into use, the etiquette in vogue at time, as I supposed, not requiring them. I returned to the chapel, philosophizing on the wonderful fruitfulness of the land of promise into which I had come, of which I was now an inhabitant, and where other surprises were awaiting me.

SOCIAL ENJOYMENT.

The house I had rented, stood upon wooden blocks, the floor being about two feet above the ground. The space underneath the floor, hollowed out to some depth, and partly filled with stagnant water, afforded a delightful retreat to the hogs of the neighboring farms, on their frequent sallies into town on pleasure bent. Having recited my office and said my beads, I was in happy anticipation of peaceful slumber, when my attention was aroused by a fresh accession of visitors to the underground story, who seemed to come rather as invaders than as friends to the parties in possession. Soon a more than usual racket of biting, squealing and grunting went on, which, together with the unbearable odor of the place, had an unnerving effect upon me. Yet I might possibly have held the fort and been victor in the end, had not a new and unexpected attack in force been made on me. The master hog of the place, a huge fellow, adjusting his itchy back to the floor under my feet, his bristles sticking up between the boards, gave me and my little chapel such a rocking and shaking, that I thought the end of the world had come. Realizing that the abomination of desolation was in the holy place, I fled, not to the mountains, for they were not near, but into the woods which were close by. How I spent the wearisome night I do not know. In the morning, however, feeling that that there was yet a little life in me, I went, meek and humble, to the poor railroad men and told them my sad story. They pitied me very much, and forthwith went to work and built a log shanty for me, so that I was soon domiciled amongst them. The priest's shanty was almost twelve feet square, built of unhewn sticks and limbs of trees, laid over each other for walls, to a height of about eight feet. Openings were made in the wooden walls for a door and window, which, as likewise the floor and roof, were of undressed plank from a neighboring saw-mill. Bedstead, table and chairs, were of like fashion and material. I taught catechism and said the rosary and night prayers in the shanty, where also I entertained visitors, who were not a few, whether on business or curiosity. I was a favorite with the railroad civil engineers, a pleasant class of gentlemen who often came late at night seeking shelter under the community roof, as there was no hotel in town. The difficulty was not overwhelming when my friends came one at a time, which was seldom, but when they came in twos and threes, as was usually the case, and not being able to solve the hotel problem of putting twelve guests into eleven rooms and giving each of them a room, the readier method was adopted, of giving them up heads and points to Morpheus. Gradually under careful consideration of the situation, I became suspicious of Center Point. My ideas, brightened by experience, began to lead me to think, that Center Point which was not much of a place, was not to be the Center Point, as in fact it never came to be; the coveted destiny being in abeyance for Brookfield the center point to come.

JOHN THE BAPTIST.

Keeping my convictions to myself, I asked and got the loan of a horse, from Mr. Patrick Tooey, a good hearted Irishman, a Catholic, a contractor on the railroad. "The horse I give you," he said, "seems to have been intended for you. Your name is John, as I know. Your patron saint is very likely St. John the Baptist. This horse is John the Baptist. He was so-called by his late owner of whom I bought him—a Baptist preacher in these backwoods here." I felt a shudder at the irreverence of calling an animal by so sacred a name. And yet that name gave me fresh courage. I felt that my heavenly patron St. John the Baptist, whom I had followed in a measure into the wilderness, would lead me to some place where I could do some good. At the end of a day's journey devoid of definite purpose, I found myself entering a delightful little town, charmingly situated in an open prairie surrounded by woods. It was Chillicothe, a place of about one thousand inhabitants.

CHILLICOTHE.

I put up at the city hotel, the only hostelry in town. It was a dark-painted, dust-covered, small frame building, with a shaky little porch over the front. But it was an important place. All the great four-horse mail stages, the boudoir Pullman coaches of the West in those days, made it headquarters for receiving and dismissing passengers, loading and unloading mail and express, and changing horses, and great was the gaping crowd of unkempt urchins and rustic citizens in homespun that greeted each stage arrival. Next day, after careful observation and inquiry, but without disclosing my character or missionary purpose, I found that the townspeople, white and black, were mostly Kentuckians, and that the prevailing religious beliefs were: Baptist, Methodist, Presbyterian and Campbellite; each having a separate church, with more or less aristocratic membership and pervading influence. It was well known, however, that there was one Catholic in town, a lady of education, refined manners and retiring disposition, the wife of a non-Catholic, a prominent lawyer—the family being favorably spoken of.

A CONGREGATION OF ONE.

I lost no time presenting myself to my congregation, this said lady, who received me courteously and introduced me to her husband and children. I was invited by her to say Mass at her house, which I did on the following day. She and her children assisted at Mass, at which, having prepared herself by confession, she received Holy Communion. The children, too, were soon baptized; those of them of age to learn, having been taught the prayers and catechism by their pious mother. But the good family was in great pecuniary straits at the time. The lawyer's business not proving lucrative in so new and backward a place, he was obliged to mortgage his residence, and the mortgage overdue was about to be foreclosed. I was earnestly besought to save the family, if in my power to do so, from being turned out homeless in the street. After some consideration I did not see how I could not do what was in my power in such a case. The sum needed did not much exceed two hundred dollars, but that amount would take the last dollar I could command. The mortgage was lifted. The providential relief of a distressed worthy family opened for me a chapel and a temporary home, though a poor one. The husband became a good Catholic. The children grew up pious and good, and one of them became a Sister of Charity. The church did not suffer, although the few dollars given away, were much needed to help so poor a foundation.

THE PRIEST IN TOWN.

When it became known that there was a priest in town, great was the curiosity to see him. It was supposed he should be an elderly man, of grave, austere appearance. Some who had seen him, said he was a young man and by no means austere. Strangers, young and old, who entered the town, were eyed closely as they passed by. Some averred that a showman, entering town, clad in fine raiment, and riding a dappled white and bay horse, was mistaken for the priest. The priest, however, could not long keep himself within the cloud. When he came to be known, he was found to be a tall thin man, wearing plain black travel-stained clothes; and his horse was not a dappled prancing steed, but a plain little sorrel pacer. The next craze was to see the priest in his vestments and to hear what he had to say. As there was no Catholic church in town, the surmises were various, as to which of the Protestant churches he would exhibit himself in. The non-Catholics, however, took care that he should get none of their churches, and they were not without having been asked, but not by the priest, for the favor. Ed. Darlington, editor of an able and very independent little paper then published at Chillicothe, had much to say of the preachers, and in no very complimentary strain, on the subject of their refusal. And to show them that the priest did not stand in need of their churches, he got the use of the Court House, and had it cleaned and fitted up for the priest to lecture in. He, moreover, attended the priest's lectures, and liberally advertised them free of charge. At the close of the lectures, which were continued every evening for a week, John Graves, the oldest citizen and the first settler in the town, donated a lot to the priest to build a church on. The lot was surveyed and staked out by George H. Nettleton, the eminent citizen and great railroad president and manager, then a young man of prepossessing manners, appearance and address, a division engineer on the construction of the Hannibal and St. Joseph railroad, and for the moment engaged in laying out John Graves' urban farm into streets and town lots.

CHAPTER III.

HAVING concluded, as Divine Providence seemed to have directed, to make Chillicothe my central mission station, I naturally began to inquire whether there were any Catholic settlers in the surrounding country; for, so far as I had gone, I had found none, except the few transient laborers working here and there along the line of the Hannibal and St. Joseph railway. Having heard of Sullivan County, I imagined, as the name seemed to suggest, that it might be perhaps a Catholic settlement. I determined to go there. Inquiring how to go to Milan–the county seat–I was told that there was no direct way to it, and that the best way was to go by the county road eastward to Linneus twenty-five miles, and thence northward to Milan thirty miles. To avoid tiring the horse lent to me, and to save myself the fatigue of so long a journey on horseback, I hired a buggy and span of horses, making an afternoon journey from Chillicothe to Linneus, and a forenoon journey the next day from Linneus to Milan. Approaching Milan, with its few and primitive dwellings in sight, I was suddenly and without previous notice, brought to a stop, by the wild behavior of a disorderly crowd of young men and boys, dressed in ragged jeans and coon-skin caps, seemingly under the influence of liquor, who with boisterous language were firing volleys of rifle shots across my way, from the woods on one side of the road where they were standing, against a target fastened to a tree on the other side. The crashing and whizzing of the bullets so terrified my horses that I could not proceed. Crouching in the buggy and reining my horses around, I was soon in full retreat and at a faster gait than I advanced on Milan, having supposed from what I saw and as I afterwards learned, that there were no Catholics in the place. Through the afternoon and the waning hours of evening, not having rested or refreshed myself or my horses the whole day, I kept on widening the distance between myself and the Milanese. At nightfall, having recrossed Locust Creek and re-entered Linn county, despairing of being able to reach Linneus that night, I turned off from the county road, and took a smaller road that led to a farm house in sight some distance to the left.

TRUE NOBILITY.

Soon I was in front of the farm house, before a rail fence over which was a wooden stile. Inside the fence, before the door of the house, was a pile of wood, trunks and limbs of trees, some of it cut short for the fire place. The house was a one-story one-room log building, having smaller log buildings

and some porches against its sides and angles. The
man of the house seeing me—a stranger at the door,
tying my horses to the fence, went out to meet me,
and saluting me asked me very kindly, if he could be
of assistance to me. I told him I was on my way
towards Linneus, that having travelled a long distance
that day, I and my horses were tired, and could go
no farther, and that I would accept his very great
kindness, if he would keep me and my horses on his
place that night, and that we needed food and rest.
He replied "Yes, sir, come in; under such circumstances we never refuse to keep a stranger with us.
But our accommodations are not of the best. We
will give you as good as we have, and we hope you
will not be dissatisfied with us." I thanked him
very sincerely and assured him I would be for ever
grateful to him. He at once began unhitching my
horses, to which I respectfully objected, saying I
could not allow him to be my servant, especially as
he had already overcome me by his kindness. "But,
you are tired," he said, "please go into the house
and rest; I will water and feed your horses as carefully as I would my own, and I venture to say you
will find them in good condition to travel in the
morning." I obeyed, and on entering the house
bowed modestly to those present. The lady of the
house welcomed me, and offering me a chair
bade me be seated. She said the family had taken
supper, but that in a little while a supper would be

prepared for me. I had not long to wait. A well cooked abundant supper was soon set before me, of which I heartily partook; the lady and her children— sons and daughters, looking on and seemingly quite pleased that I had made myself much at home with them.

AN AFTER-SUPPER COLLOQUY.

After supper my good friend, the man of the house, engaged me in conversation.

"May I ask you, sir, your name?"

"My name, sir, is Hogan."

"You said you were going to Linneus. Linneus is our county seat. I know almost every one in Linneus, but I have not seen you there. I suppose you do not live in Linneus?"

"Indeed, sir, I am a stranger in Linneus, and in this part of the state. Being on a journey towards Linneus, I hoped to get there before night, but failed to do so, my horses being tired."

"I see you are not accustomed to work, as I may judge by your appearance; your hands and clothes do not show that you follow the plough as I do."

"True, sir: though not accustomed to work, I nevertheless regard farm work as a very honorable occupation."

"You may be a doctor, then?"

"No, indeed, sir. The practice of medicine is a very responsible profession, and I have not aspired to it."

"Perhaps you are a lawyer, and going to Linneus to open a law office?"

"No, sir; the practice of law is not to my taste, and, besides, I have not ability enough to enter that profession."

"What then, may your calling be?"

"Indeed, sir, I have no worldly calling in particu lar. I am a young man, not long out of college. I was told that North Missouri was, as I find it is, a beautiful country, and I am seeking a place to settle in it, if perchance, I may be suited."

"May I ask, where have you journeyed from to-day?"

"I have come from Milan this afternoon. I passed by here this morning, going to Milan from Linneus. Yesterday in the afternoon I travelled from Chillicothe to Linneus. At Chillicothe I have been staying some days, having travelled there from St. Louis, which I may call my home."

"As you have mentioned Chillicothe, is it not a great place for churches and preachers?"

"There are several churches and preachers in Chillicothe, as I have been told."

Has there not been a great controversy there lately between the Methodists and Universalists? Have you attended it?"

"No, indeed, sir; I have not attended the controversy. To my mind, it is too late now to discuss the question, as to which of the churches has the

true religion. We now cannot be very reliable witnesses of facts that took place nearly two thousand
years ago, and if the Christians of the first ages have
not settled that question, it would seem useless for
us to try to do so. Besides, I do not see how preachers, now-a-days, can tell us anything not already
known on the subject of religion.

THE UNIVERSALISTS, WHAT DO YOU THINK OF THEM?

"But what do you think of these Universalists?"

"Their doctrine, sir, if I understand it, seems
strange to me. I had always thought that there was
a difference between right and wrong, virtue and
vice, righteousness and unrighteousness; but according to the Universalists, there would seem to be no
difference, at least so far as the consequences of acts
of whatever kind are concerned, since they say that
a bad man is as well off in the end as a good man,
that sinfulness ends in righteousness as much as
sanctity, that Judas impenitent and the Impenitent
Thief are in Heaven as well as St. Peter and St. John
the Baptist. If this be so, the virtues we prize most,
that truly make men great, and that are necessary to
uphold morals in society, are no better than empty
names; for why should we be honest, or chaste, or
pious, or merciful, if these heroic virtues be nothing;
and who will venture to say they are nothing? To
me it would seem, that man must be created again
different from what he is, and that society must be
re-cast and on a new plan, before what the Univer-

salists say can be true. "

"That suits me. That is my doctrine out and out."

"I thank you. I feel quite flattered, that you approve of my humble opinions."

THE OLD PRIEST, WHAT DO YOU THINK OF HIM?

"But what do you think of these people called Papists? The old priest comes along regularly, down here on the railroad, and pretends to forgive sins. The Papists confess their sins to him, and give him lots of money to be forgiven. The old priest goes away, and as soon as he is gone, the Papists are as wicked as before. What do you think of that?"

"It seems strange indeed. But, upon reflection, since the people pay their lawyers, doctors and preachers, I suppose in like manner, the Papists may be allowed to pay their priests."

"But don't you see the wickedness of cheating the people out of their money, by pretending to forgive them their sins?"

"True, in that light, it would be a wicked thing. But, it is more than likely that Papists do not see it in that light. For myself, I will not say that I am much of a religious or learned man. Nevertheless, I will say that I read a little in the Bible, and that I found there these words spoken by Christ to His Apostles: 'Whose sins ye shall forgive, they are forgiven them.' Papists believe that by these words christ communicated power to His Apostles to forgive sins. And because Christ said that He would be with His Apostles until the end of the world, these Apostles must be in the world yet, because the world has not yet come to an end. These Apostles, that is, the ordained ministers of Christ, whoever they be, have this power to-day as fully as when Christ first gave it. This is the belief of the Papists in regard to their priests, and the reason no doubt, why they go to the priest to forgive them their sins. In fact it would seem to be a belief as true as the Bible itself. In other respects, too, it would seem a reasonable belief, and one that is practised every day in our state affairs. For instance, the Governor of this state is Bob Stewart. Bob Stewart is said to be not a very exemplary citizen. In fact, as I believe, it is well known, that he drinks quite freely, and is often so under the influence of drink as not to be able to attend to his official duties. Nevertheless, should Bob Stewart, governor of this state as he is, go at any time to the state penitentiary, and say to the warden of that penitentiary: 'Warden, there are three men here that I pardon, one of them is a murderer, another is a robber, and the third is a horse-thief; I pardon these, let these go;' are they not by his words, then and there expressed fully pardoned, and their sins against the state forgiven them? And if the state of Missouri can, and does, give the power to forgive sins, to one of its citizens, and he by no means the best or worthiest citizen, to be exercised for purposes of mercy; why may not Almighty God

give a like power for a like purpose, even to an un-
worthy man, such as people say the old priest is?
For myself, I will say, that I have often meditated
much on this matter, and the conclusion I have come
to, is, that this must be the reason why Catholics believe that the priest can forgive sins."

"I thank you, sir, for this explanation which is
very interesting and which never occurred to my
mind in such light before. Perhaps, after all, if we
could understand the priests and the Papists, they
might not be such as we think they are."

RETIRING TO REST.

It was now a considerable time after supper, and
the good man of the house, seeing I was tired, suggested to the members of the family who sat around
listening, that they retire to rest. The room in
which we were, the largest one in the house, had a
bed, some chairs, a table, two woollen wheels, a loom
for weaving, and a large fire-place with board mantel. I was provided with a light and shown into a
small comfortable apartment, which, though quite
plain was very clean. I need not say, that after my
long and fatiguing day's journey, I was in want of
sleep which I very much enjoyed.

DEPARTING IN WONDER

In the morning, quite refreshed by a sound sleep,
and having partaken of a good breakfast, I was told
that my horses had been watered and fed, and that
they were fresh and in good order to resume their

journey. It took but a short time to harness them to the buggy, in which I took my seat, whip and reins in hand. Having inquired of my host, what my expenses were. He named a modest sum, which I paid him, and at the same time thanked him most sincerely. At parting I said to him, "My dear sir, I assure you, your kindness to me I will never forget, and I hope it may come to be in my power to serve you as kindly as you have served me. May the good God bless and reward you, and lead you unto all that is good. Furthermore, my dear friend, I have to say to you, not knowing how you may regard it, whether as an honor or otherwise, that you entertained a Catholic priest last night. I am the Catholic priest who attends the railroad men in the southern part of this county. My dear friend, I hope to see you again. Once more I say, God bless you. Good-bye." The horses pulled on their tugs, and moved away briskly. When I had gone quite a distance, I looked back, my host was still standing, where I left him, as if fixed to the ground, gazing steadily after me. I passed through Linneus before mid-day, and in the evening reached Chillicothe.

CHAPTER IV.

IRISH BROWN.

ALTHOUGH the record of my journey to Milan was not as favorable as I expected, I nevertheless resolved to continue my inquiries in other directions. I had heard of a man named Irish Brown, a farmer living in the north-west part of Linn county, who as his name and nationality would indicate, might be a Catholic. I determined to look for him. Everyone in Linn and Livingston counties had heard of Irish Brown, but no one that I met could tell me exactly where he lived. I made one fruitless journey endeavoring to find him. A second time I was successful. I found him owning and cultivating a large well-improved farm, having a good residence on it, at the head of Parson Creek, about eighteen miles northeast of Chillicothe. He was a native of Dublin, and his wife a native of Kentucky. They were good Catholics, and blessed with several children; some grown, some small, but most of them unbaptized. They were rejoiced to see a priest. I said Mass at their house, and baptized the children. At parting, I made appointment to visit them occasionally.

JOHN THE BAPTIST AGAIN.

From Linn and Livingston I went westward through Grundy and Daviess counties, but found no Catholics except one family, temporarily residing at Gallatin. From Gallatin I went southwest into De Kalb county, and thence south and south-east into Clinton and Caldwell counties. On this journey, I proceeded by easy stages on horseback, as John the Baptist was weighted down, less by the rider than the large satchel and saddlebags, containing vestments, chalice, missal, altar-stone, and other necessaries for the mission. Crossing Grind Stone Creek, a tributary of Grand River, flowing in a northerly direction, in the southeast part of De Kalb county, at about mid-day, the weather being warm, I permitted John, my namesake, to wade in past knee deep, and dropping the bridle loose on his neck, I let him stoop down to drink. Having drunk to his content, delighted with the clear, cool water, he sat down leisurely, leaning over on one side and keeping his head above water. I went over too, endeavoring all the while, to keep my head, as the horse did, above water. We were both in the Jordan. I hastened to get out of it. He seemed in no hurry to finish the ceremony. The whole occurrence was so ludicrous, and the Baptist evidently so well up to it, that my sides shook with laughter. As the weather was dry and the sun bright and warm, the books and vestments, spread out on the grassy prairie, soon regained their former good condition. The poor missionary, however, very meekly submitted to the drying process, his raiment remaining on his back. Soon, all put to rights again, I was once more on the move, endeavoring to reach the hamlet of Mirabile before nightfall, the place being then fully fifteen miles distant.

THE HAMLET OF MIRABILE.

Mirabile, situated on the confines of Caldwell and Clinton counties, was known to have some resident Catholic families. A Catholic of means and business capacity had found his way there among its first settlers. Purchasing some land, which he tilled, and carrying on a country store in which he prospered, he was soon considered a rising business man. His two oldest children, daughters, whom he educated well, or as best he could, married non-Catholics, one of whom was a successful physician, and the other in course of time became Governor of the State. Around these clustered some acquaintances, likewise farmers, also good Catholics, about seven families in all. They were glad to see me and received me kindly. I said Mass for them, staying there about two days. I suggested to them to build a church in their midst, and that I would aid them to the best of my power. My proposition was not favorably received. The old gentleman said: "Reverend Father, we are happy to welcome you here, and to have the opportunity to hear Mass and receive the Sacraments. We have

deemed it best that this be done, not in an open and
public manner, but privately amongst ourselves, and
within the precincts of our dwellings. There is
much prejudice here to us as Catholics and against
our Church, and this prejudice, if aroused by any
public ceremony or display on our part, may be
taken as a challenge and in very bad spirit by our
non-Catholic friends. It is better, as I think, for
these reasons, and because there are so few of us
here, and our means very limited, that the building
of a church be not thought of at present." The
other Catholics who stood by, listening, expressed
opinions agreeing with his. There was no hope of
building a church at Mirabile.

DISCOURAGEMENT

Discouragement and disappointment heavier than
before, fell on me and brooded over my mind.
Throughout all North Missouri, so far as I had travelled, there was not one Catholic Church, or hope of
one. True, indeed, a lot of ground had been offered
for a church in Chillicothe. But whence wherewith
to build? The poor railroad laborers, good Catholics,
were very generous, and could be depended upon to
give of their slender means, for this purpose. But
they, too, were now, alas, at great disadvantage.
Distress and disappointment had come to stare them
in the face. The banks throughout the United States
had just failed. Credit was everywhere broken. Public works everywhere suspended. The disastrous fi-

nancial crash of 1857 was on the face of the country —a dark over-hanging cloud that took many a day to dispell. I returned quite disheartened to Chillicothe, where, having rested a day or two, I set out for Center Point, to return John the Baptist to his owner, and to communicate the information, that, as it seemed best to do, I would in future make my home at Chillicothe.

CHAPTER V

MAIN PURPOSE NOT ADVANCED.

SO far my main purpose in setting out from St. Louis to find a place where Catholics might settle on land, was not advanced any. My inquiries, wherever I had travelled through North Missouri, led to the information, that the Government land in that region of country, had all been sold, or given away to railroads, and that the present owners held it at high price; about twenty dollars an acre for improved land, and for unimproved land about ten dollars an acre, which sum absolutely prohibited purchase by poor people, such as Catholic emigrants mostly were.

ABNORMAL.

And here may be briefly considered the condition of Catholic emigrants in Missouri, which I had ample opportunity to know. During the years 1854-55 on the mission at St. John's church, St. Louis, I observed that the Catholic servant girls attending that church, were not less than three hundred or more. They were regular monthly communicants, usually going to confession Saturday night after supper, their day's work being then done, and to Holy Communion on Sunday morning at five o'clock

Mass, which was celebrated for them at that early hour, so that they could return in time to prepare breakfast for their non-Catholic employers not yet risen from their beds. And the number of Catholic girls attending several other Catholic churches in St. Louis, was even much greater than at St. John's. The Catholic young men, likewise for the most part emigrants from Ireland, not finding work in the cities, and there being no work for them on farms in competition with slave labor, were obliged to seek employment on the railroads, and to live in camps and move from place to place, as the shifting nature of their employment required. The total separation of these emigrants, one party not finding employment where the other did, was in a most anomalous condition, resulting in practically debarring them from intermarriage, and from marriage of whatever sort, since they could not, without sacrifice of principle, intermarry with those habituated to deride their Christian faith, or who regarded marriage as only a civil contract to be dissolved under frivolous pretexts for divorce, that served but to open a way for marriage infidelity and licentiousness. To their honor, be it said, that sooner than degrade marriage to the sacrilegious level of a mere civil contract—alike destructive of religion and society, they chose to decline altogether the formation of family ties that would but lead to a dishonored posterity and an unchristian civilization.

THE REMEDY.

Profoundly impressed with these facts, it seemed to me to be my duty to do whatever might be in my power, to aid these people to rise from their condition of servitude, to ownership and cultivation of land, so as to secure for them, beyond doubt, a settled and permanent mode of existence, that would accord better with their higher social aspirations and religious principles. This, however, could not be done in North Missouri, where land was held at too high a price. I had heard that there were still remaining unsold large tracts of government land in southern Missouri, that could be bought for one dollar an acre, and some of it for a less price; and that it was of a moderate fertility, though much inferior to the land in North Missouri. One dollar an acre seemed to me, to be within the possible reach of comparatively poor people. Having procured from the district land office at Jackson, Cape Girardeau county, Missouri, plots and surveys of wide tracts of vacant government lands in the said region of country, I lost no time setting out and journeying to see these lands.

SURVEYING.

Travelling by way of Brunswick, Jefferson City, St. Louis, Old Mines, Potosi, Iron Mountain and Frederick Town, I halted at Greenville, in Wayne county, where I hired a surveyor familiar with the country. I examined the lands on the head waters of Little Black River, Cane Creek, Brushy Creek, in

Ripley (now Carter) county, and entered four hundred and eighty acres in a body on Ten Mile Creek, making arrangements at once to put men thereon, opening and cultivating it. With the surveyor I rode westward, across the Current River, by Van Buren, up Pike Creek, thence southward over the great divide east of Eleven Points River as far as the head waters of Buffalo Creek, thence eastward along Buffalo Creek and its tributaries to a ford on Current River. At this place there was a mill and homestead owned and occupied by a man named Appollinaris Tucker; he and his family were the only Catholics known to be residing at that time in that district. At the time of my arrival, Mrs. Tucker was in the last stages of her mortal illness, in which it seemed God's Holy Will that she should linger until her longings could be gratified to receive the last Sacraments; and, as it happened, from the hands of the first priest known to have come into that region of country. After Mrs. Tucker's death, I returned homewards, by way of Iron Mountain, St. Louis, and Hannibal, to Chillicothe.

MY DEAR FRIEND FATHER FOX.

Arrived at Chillicothe, I corresponded without delay, with my dear friend and worthy brother priest, Rev. James Fox, rector of St. Joachim's church, Old Mines, Missouri, who as I well knew, was deeply concerned for the matter of land ownership and occupancy by Catholic emigrants. The incidents of my late journey, which I related to him, so interested him that he requested to be permitted to accompany me on another such journey, if I should have occasion to make one. I wrote to him to be ready and that I would soon call on him. Before many days, and in the latter part of November, we set out together on horseback from Old Mines. Travelling by way of Caledonia and Edgehill, we passed through Centerville the county seat of Reynolds county. Thence entering Shannon County, we descended Blair Creek, remarkable for its alternate lime-stone and red porphyry hills. Afterwards, we crossed the Current River at the mouth of Jack's Fork, thence to Eminence, thence to Birch Tree, thence to Thomasville, thence to Pike Creek, thence to Van Buren, thence to Ten Mile Creek, thence to Black River, thence by way of Otter Creek, McKenzie Creek and Big Creek, through Caledonia and Potosi, homeward. Reynolds county we found entirely unfit for settlement, not one tenth of the land being tillable. Shannon and Oregon counties had much tillable land, perhaps one-third of the whole area, but none of it of prime quality except the river alluvial bottoms. Everywhere through these two last named counties, there was good stock range and abundance of valuable pine forest

RETURNED to Chillicothe in December, I continued as before, seeking and visiting Catholic settlers and railroad camps, saying Mass and administering Sacraments wherever I found Catholics. Some incidents will give an idea of the simple and affecting scenes of my missionary labors in those days.

Travelling across the tributaries of Van Dusen Creek in the south-east part of Linn county, I noticed smoke rising from a little cabin, not much higher than the brambles and rosinweeds by which it was surrounded. Approaching, I knocked slightly on the board roof of the little house. A lady's voice spoke "Come in." Entering, I found two little children and their mother. After a word or two of salutation and inquiry, she said her husband had gone away some distance looking for employment. I could suspect from her manner and conversation that she was a Catholic. I told her I was a priest. and I gave her my name. The news gave her great joy. She said she and her husband were Catholics, that their children were as yet unbaptized, that they came to Missouri, having lately left a remote district in

Illinois, where there was no Catholic Church. As she expressed a wish to have her children baptized, I immediately began getting my ritual, stole, and surplice ready, to administer the Sacrament. Soor there was a halt. "Where are the sponsors," said I. She replied there were none near, and that if it would not be too long to wait, she would send her husband, upon his return home, to look for sponsors, although she did not know that he could find any. I could not wait, not knowing how long it might be before sponsors could be got. Neither could I go away, leaving the children unbaptized. I proceeded with the ceremony, and when the moment came for the baptism, taking the children one after another from the hands of their mother, I put them in turn on my knee and baptized them. Then I continued my journey.

DYING IN A COLD CABIN.

Not far from there, travelling along the railroad line, at a point where work was seemingly suspended, I was passing by an apparently deserted shanty, into which, however, I happened to look, not supposing anyone to be in such a place. To my surprise, I saw several little children, poorly clad, crawling on the bare earthen floor, and near them, or a sort of bed made of sticks and twigs covered with hay, a woman lying speechless and in the agony of death. There was no fire in the little cabin which seemed like a deserted stable. Through the oper door and the wide open chinks between the logs, the cold damp wind was blowing. Each minute seemed likely to be the last for the poor mother. And the perishing little ones on the floor, too young to know anything of their sad condition, gave symptoms by their cries that death would soon end their miseries likewise. Convinced from all the circumstances that she belonged to one of the railroad camps, I tried to arouse her to consciousness, but my effort was in vain. Kneeling by her bedside, I gave her Absolution, Extreme Unction, and the Plenary Indulgence, Then going as fast as I could to the railroad camp about two miles distant, I informed the people there of the deplorable condition of the poor family in the open stable, on the river bank, near the hill side. They had known of such a family, but had thought that the husband was in care of them. Hastening to the place, they arrived in time to see the poor woman die. The children were saved however. The husband had gone forty miles away looking for work. When he returned, his little children were cared for by strangers, and his beloved wife was lying near by in the woods in her grave.

BORN IN A STABLE.

About sixty miles west of where this good lady died and lies buried, another such sad event occurred, revealing the hardships and woes to which poor emigrants were exposed in those early days, on their long journeys in search of homes. A very decent and pious Catholic family that had been settled for years on a farm in Wisconsin, sold their lands and homestead there to better their condition. In a tent-covered wagon drawn by a pair of good horses, the father and mother and young children, accompanied by an elderly lady, a relative of the family, travelled day after day on their long journey of four hundred miles, towards their place of destination, the neighborhood of which they reached as the last piercing winds of March were passing away, with a light covering of snow on the ground. In a deep and sheltered hollow at a place called McDonald's Branch, in the north-west corner of Caldwell county, the good father of the family finding a log house or stable unoccupied which seemed to have no owner, availed himself of the opportunity presented, to make use of it as a temporary residence or resting place for his family during a hasty journey he intended to make to his late home, to make final disposal of some business there. He had not gone far, when a great trouble befell his little family. The dear mother of his children gave birth to twins, far away from human habitation, and without the necessary care that such occasion required. Death seized the mother. I was happily there in time to administer the last Sacraments to her. Next I baptized the two little babes. The stable scene reminding me of Bethlehem, I called them Joseph and Mary. So sweet and helpless seemed the little angels to me, that I felt strongly moved to fold them in my cloak within my arms and take them away, But God who loved them much more than I could, had a place in heaven waiting for them. They too soon passed away to the fond embraces of their loving mother in a better world. Mother and children lie buried in one grave. God and His Angels are looking down forever on their sacred resting place.

CHAPTER VII.

REV. William Walsh, the devoted zealous pastor of St. Peter's church, Jefferson City, ever a loving faithful friend of the emigrant, took the greatest possible interest in every effort made to lead the good Catholic Irish people from the railroad shanties and the back streets and cellars of the cities, to locate them on lands. With this purpose in view, he offered to accompany me on my next journey into southern Missouri, so that having knowledge of the country and of the progress of the undertaking in which I was interested, he could aid me, if in his power, to do so. We set out from St. Louis together in the last days of January, 1858. Travelling on the Iron Mountain Railroad to its southern terminus, then somewhere in Washington County, we thence proceeded on horseback, following somewhat, but diverging more southerly from, the route taken by Reverend Father Fox and myself a short time previous. At Van Buren we found a Canadian named Ronge, a Catholic, whose three children I baptized. Going eastward from there we crossed the Black River at its junction with Brushy Creek. Reverend Father Walsh when crossing the river, although keeping his feet raised as high as possible along the horses sides, still could not keep them entirely out of the water, which was deep and very cold, it being freezing weather at the time. The result was bad for the dear Reverend Father. The only change of clothing which we had was a pair of socks, which he put on instead of the wet ones. These did not save him. The cold wet boots and the wet frozen clothing brought on a chill which was soon followed by coughing and fever. Next, the flushed face and the short, difficult breathing with other symptoms of pneumonia, came on apace. We diverged from our intended course and made by the shortest way for Greenville, the county seat of Wayne county, where we hoped to find some kind of hotel accommodation. For some days the dear Reverend Father lay in danger of death, in a poor uncomfortable tavern, and under the care of an unskilful physician. Soon, however, he began to recover and by degrees grew better so as to be past all danger, for which merciful favor I was most grateful to Almighty God. During his convalescence I made a journey to Jackson in Cape Girardeau county, to employ an agent near the Land Office there, to transact business for the settlers. Returned to Greenville, I was glad to find my dear reverend friend in much better health and courage than when I had left him. We again set out together and rode by easy stages towards the Iron Mountain and Potosi, thence homeward by rail to St.

Louis; he going to Jefferson City and I to Chillicothe.

The information we had gathered was, that Ripley,
Oregon and Howell counties afforded good advan-
tages for settlement to people of small means and of
patient, frugal, industrious habits. The country as
we found, was quite healthy. Land was cheap. The
land was by no means all good, but enough of it was
good to support many inhabitants, if not a dense pop-
ulation. About one-third of the whole area could be
tilled for orchards, vineyards, or the usual vegetable
or cereal crops; and the yield was far more generous
than the appearance of the soil would indicate. The
ground, too, when once broken and cleared, was easily
cultivated. There was plenty of timber of good
quality everywhere at hand, that made it an easy task
to build dwellings, barns, stables, fences, and to furnish fuel. Springs and streams of pure, clear water
were abundant except in a few localities. The lands
that could not be cultivated were fairly grassy and
could feed many cattle. The price of government
land was from twelve and a half cents to one dollar
and twenty five cents per acre. The best cultivated
lands, of which there were many farms along the
rivers and streams, with houses, stables, barns and
fences, could be bought for ten dollars an acre, buildings and improvements included. Some could be
bought for five, and some even for three dollars an
acre. These prices were much lower than for unim-

proved land in North Missouri. The winters, too, were longer and severer in northern Missouri than in southern Missouri. Likewise, the scarcity or total want of timber for fuel, fencing and building purposes, made it impossible for a poor man, or for a man not comparatively wealthy, to acquire and improve land in North Missouri. All things considered, there was no reason whatever to doubt, that emigrants who could not own land in their native countries, however much they desired to do so, and who as renters maintained themselves there even on small patches of barren land, could by using the same thrift and energy in southern Missouri, successfully cultivate land, and establish on it for themselves and their posterity a permanent homestead.

LAND OFFICES AND LAND SURVEYORS.

The proposed settlement, and the district of country of its intended location becoming better known, there were many applicants for land entries. In order that these entries should be as satisfactory as possible, a knowledge by actual observation of each tract and of its metes and bounds, was first of all necessary. This indispensable knowledge was to be obtained only by the services of competent surveyors familiar with the topography of the country, and practically acquainted with the United States system of land surveys and subdivisions. Such surveyors were engaged, and with them were sent competent assistants. Their duties required them to

travel from place to place, making examinations, surveys and field notes of government vacant lands; the
vacant tracts being designated on maps furnished
them from time to time, on application to the land
office. In correspondence with these surveyors in
the field, a competent agent near the land office was
employed to present applications for entries of land,
make payment therefor, and procure certificates of
entry in the names of the intending owners. To
meet the expenses of these several agencies and other
incidental outlays, a charge additional to the price of
the land was made to purchasers. This charge would
have been sufficient, had there been no competitive
land seeking at the time. As matters went, people
from the eastern and middle states, as well as Missourians, had their agents and surveyors selecting and
applying for land; and many made land entries at
random and without any attempt at selection or examination. In the rush for land, applicants upon
entering their names on the books of the land office,
with the description of the land wanted, had often to
wait months for their turn to come following the
hundreds before them. Usually, too, the information
long waited for, was disappointing; the land asked
for, and that was vacant when the application was
made, having been reached sooner by persons more
forward on the lists. From this cause the surveyors'
work and charges were often lost, at the expense of
the applicant, and sometimes thrice over in succes-

sion, the cost increasing with each disappointment. Soon, to gratify the wishes of applicants, and because nothing better could be done, entries of some kind of land were made, and hundreds of applications were returned, no land whatever having been entered. The following extracts from letters of the agent for the colony, near the land office, give some idea of the difficulties that existed.

"JACKSON, Mo., APRIL 15, 1858.

The South West ¼ Section 7, and the North West ¼ of the North West ¼ Section 12, Township 26 North, Range 3 East, embraced in Maurice O'Brien's application, was sold in February last. A wrong marking of the plats showed the above tracts vacant. The South ½ Section 1, Township 26 North, Range 2 East, embraced in James Evans' application, has also been sold. You will please furnish other tracts in lieu of the above. Very respectfully,

G. W. FERGUSON."

"JACKSON, Mo., APRIL 26, 1858.

The land embraced in James Burke's application, to wit; the South-East ¼ and South ½ of North East ¼, Section 17, Township 26 North, Range 3 East, has been entered by another person. All of Section 17 has been sold.

Very respectfully, G. W. FERGUSON."

"JACKSON, Mo., APRIL 30, 1858.

I find from examination that the following tracts, applied for by you, have been sold, to-wit; application of James Murray, North West ¼, and lot 1 North East ¼, Section 6; application of Denis Sullivan, South West ¼, Section 21; application of Denis Hurley, South West ¼ Section 24; application of Thomas Mulvehille, South East ¼, Section 22; application of Michael Mara, North ½, Section 22; application of Stephen McNamara, West ½, Section 23; application of Patrick Griffin, South ½ of North East ¼, Section 36;

application of Patrick Rowe, North West ¼, Section 30. All these have been sold to others.

                        Very respectfully, G. W. FERGUSON.'

At this stage the land entry business was turned over entirely to A. & D. O'Brien, Agents, 38 Chestnut street, St. Louis; thereby leaving me free to attend exclusively to my missionary duties.

CHAPTER VIII

CHURCH BUILDING AT CHILLICOTHE.

I NOW turned my attention to the erection of the church at Chillicothe, for which I had got a site some time previous. The building was to be frame, seventy feet long, twenty five feet wide, eighteen feet story, with bell tower, sacristies, altar, communion rail, pews, confessional, choir gallery, and stained glass windows. I let the contract for the foundation to a man who made strong preferential claim for the job because he was a Catholic, as he said. He said, moreover, he was from Chicago, where, as he stated, he was well known, and had built much elegant masonry. The foundation wall, which was to have usual depth in the ground, was to be twenty inches above ground. It was to be built of good rubble masonry, with dressed stone along the front of the building, and hammered stone along the sides and end. Soon the stone was on the ground, of good quality, prepared according to contract, and the work was to be commenced at once. It was well known, as a matter spoken of, that I intended to be absent for some time on a missionary tour through the neighboring counties. The contractor aware of my intention, requested me to pay him in advance

for the work. He said he was out of money, that
the stone was on the ground ready, that it would be
laid in the wall in a few days, and that upon my return I would find the work done and to my entire
satisfaction. I paid him in full, and set out forthwith
on my journey. When I had left, he sold the cut
and hammered stone to be used in another building,
and then built the foundation of the church of the
cheapest stone he could find. Afterwards, skipping
from town, he sought pastures new, hoping no doubt,
in a world full of fools, soon to find another verdant
young clergyman. Arriving home, I went to inspect
the work, and found that I could kick it to pieces
with the heel of my boot. I soon, however, had the
rotten stone and crumbling wall rebuilt with better
material, and by an honester mechanic. The super-
structure was of green oak framing timbers, joists,
studding, rafters, sheathing, cut to order at a neighboring saw-mill. The weather-boarding, shingles,
flooring, doors, frames, altar and pew beards, and
boards for finishing, also nails and hardware, were
bought in St. Louis, shipped by boat to Brunswick,
and thence by a smaller boat that plied on the Grand
River, to Chillicothe landing.

CHILLICOTHE AND THE FINE ARTS.

The stained glass windows were made in St. Louis
at Miller's Stained Glass factory, thence were shipped
by boat to Hannibal, thence by rail to Shelbina, the
western terminus at the time of the Hannibal and St.

Joseph Railroad, and thence by wagon to Chillicothe, where they arrived safe, not a square inch of glass broken. Alas, the windows which were really beautiful, were not suffered to shower their rainbow tints very long over the secluded little sanctuary. A rather too warm sermon from the fervid young missionary, against forbidden secret societies, brought the gentlemen of grips and signs to visit his chapel at the midnight hour, and to belabor with barbarous sticks and guns, the artistic little gems, brought like pearls from afar, that were willing to live on and shine for God, even in the depths of the wilderness. Chillicothe's first little Catholic church had to humble itself to the level of its surroundings. Henceforward its windows were to be of vulgar glass. By great efforts, and by collections made near and far, the little church was completed. The church lot, too, was fenced, and all was paid for, so far as I knew. It was a strong tie for the hearts of Catholic people, to stop there and settle, as many of them did from that day forward.

YOU KNOW NOT THE DAY NOR THE HOUR.

And here it may not be out of place to say a word or two, on what came of the seemly duty, of providing near the church where the people came to pray, a quiet resting place for those of its members departed this life in peace with Christ. For this purpose an additional lot of ground was bought and fenced under the shadow of the church and its cross crowned steeple. To meet the expenses of this new purchase and its necessary improvements, a collection was set on foot and carried from door to door among the new comers. The first one asked for a subscription was a good Catholic of fervent faith, practical piety and humane disposition. He was blessed, too, with a faithful Catholic wife and several dear little children. "I will not be buried here," he said. "My burying place is in Springfield, Illinois, with my relatives. I mean to return there sometime, and to die and be buried there. Yet, since you are making a collection for a new cemetery, which no doubt will be needed here as elsewhere, I give you my offering. Here are five dollars for you for this purpose. I regret it is so very little, and that I am not able to give you more. I give it as an offering for the Poor Souls in Purgatory." Oh, the awful mysterious uncertainty of human life. Oh, how impenetrable the veil that hangs over our future, and that we cannot lift for one moment. "Watch ye, therefore, because you know not the day nor the hour." That evening, in company with some fellow-workmen, he went to bathe in the Grand River, and was drowned. The second day after, he was laid to rest, beside the church, the first one buried in the little cemetery he had so generously helped to purchase. God rest thee, dear christian soul. God comfort thy widow and children.

CHAPTER IX

THE completion of the little church at Chillicothe gave me opportunity to pay some attention to the many calls on me from another direction. These calls came from the settlers lately moved into southern Missouri, who claimed that I should attend them or get another priest to do so. I presented the case to His Grace the Most Reverend Archbishop of St. Louis, with request that he send a priest to take charge of the mission begun at Chillicothe, so as to leave me free to attend the new mission in southern Missouri. His Grace replied that he had not priests enough to attend the missions, that all the priests of the diocese were engaged on duties from which not one could be spared, and that, besides, he did not know that he could find a priest willing to engage in such purposes as I was in pursuit of. Not disconcerted, I resolved not to abandon either place. Without apology or explanation for going from Chillicothe, and without being able to conjecture my future movements which I placed in submission to the will of God, I set out towards the South in the end of the month of November, 1858. Travelling through the counties of Levingston, Linn,

Chariton and Randolph, I got on the cars at Sturgeon
in Boone county, which was then the terminus of the
North Missouri Railway. Arrived in St. Louis, I
took the Iron Mountain Railway cars to Pilot Knob,
and from there I travelled by wagon into southern
Missouri.

A DIFFICULTY.

Arrived at the settlement, I found a difficulty ex-
isting. In the district of country where I had bought
land the year previous, intending to make the place
the center of the proposed settlement, I found that
all the government land, fit for cultivation, had in the
meantime been bought by parties not Catholics, so
that there was no longer a possibility of owning
sufficient ground there to form a colony such as I had
contemplated. There was improved land enough in
the neighborhood that could be bought at a reasonable price and on easy conditions. But the cry was
for government land and at government price. Westward then, though very much against my will, I had
to move about forty miles, to a region of country
where there was yet much vacant government land,
on the confines of Ripley and Oregon counties, along
the tributaries of the Current and Eleven Point
rivers, about twenty miles north of the state of Arkansas.

THE NEW SETTLEMENT.

On a wide and fair tract of ground bought and
donated by Reverend James Fox of Old Mines, Mis-

souri, a one story log house forty feet square was erected and partitioned into two apartments, one for a chapel and the other for the priest's residence. Soon improvements went on apace; cutting down trees, splitting rails, burning brushwood, making fences, grubbing roots and stumps, building houses, digging wells, opening roads, breaking and ploughing land, and sowing crops. Already in the spring of 1859, there were about forty families on the newly acquired government lands, or on improved farms purchased, east and west of Current River, in the counties of Ripley and Oregon; and many more were coming, so that the settlement was fairly striding towards final success. The little chapel amid the forest trees in the wilderness was well attended. Mass, sermon, catechism, confessions, devotions, went on as in old congregations. The quiet solitariness of the place seemed to inspire devotion. Nowhere could the human soul so profoundly worship as in the depths of that leafy forest, beneath the swaying branches of the lofty oaks and pines, where solitude and the heart of man united in praise and wonder of the Great Creator.

SOCIETY IN SOUTHERN MISSOURI.

In keeping with these scenes were the simple, quiet ways of the early settlers of southern Missouri, who were mostly from North Carolina and Tennessee, and of whom much may be said in praise. They were kindhearted. honest, sincere and sociable. No stranger ever travelled amongst them without feeling his heart warmed with the fullest conviction, that, if worthy his presence gave them pleasure, that he was treated to the best they had or could afford, and that his person, money and property were safe and sacred in their keeping. Vice was little known amongst them. Intemperance was nowhere observable, although they usually took as a matter of course, their morning dram, or a drop with a friend, from a keg of the best, distilled by themselves or by some neighbor willing to share or barter on accommodating terms. Every one smoked, men and women, young and old. The WEED grew abundantly, and was usually the best tended patch of crop on the place. There was no need of manufactured tobacco or of fancy pipes. Home growth and home manufacture found favor. Corncob pipes were easily made, and for pipe stems cane was abundant. It grew along the streams and by the water's side. The maidens and swains married young, usually before twenty, often at sixteen, and their married life was remarkably virtuous and happy. The marriage dowry was usually a one room log house. The young man was fortuned by his father with a yoke of oxen and a plow. The bride was dowered by her mother with wealth of homespun dresses and household fabrics of like manufacture. Timber from a neighboring saw-mill was easily framed into a variety of articles of household furniture, and the eyes of the young

couple were none the less delighted with it, for being
pure of veneer or varnish, of which their rural surroundings gave them no knowledge whatever. Uncle
Sam had given them a homestead of three hundred
and twenty acres, at twelve and a half cents per acre.
There was no reason in the world why they should
not be happy. Moreover, the young wife had been
taught by her mother, to knit, spin, weave and sew.
The young husband had been taught by his father, to
tend sheep and cattle, and to cultivate cotton and
corn. The education of husband and wife could be
depended upon to procure them a living. The plow
cultivated plots and furrows in the field. The wheel
and loom wrought fabrics at home. There was no
need of the merchant's ship, bringing goods from
afar. No need of town fashions, or of store clothes.
Willing hands and humble hearts made the one-room
log cabin a sacred place and a happy home.

GETTING ACQUAINTED.

The old settlers were anxious to get acquainted
with the priest, many of them having travelled quite
a distance for the purpose. Their manner showed
curiosity more than prejudice towards the Catholic
Church. Many of them said, as their names indicated, and as was told them by their parents, that
they were descendants of Irish Catholics, who had
been driven or forced to emigrate in early times.
They could not explain why they were not Catholics,
as their forefathers were, except by the fact that

there were no priests or Catholic churches where they and their parents for generations were brought up. They had therefore fallen in with the prevailing churches of their surroundings. In the course of a short time, as acquaintance progressed, I was invited by some families to visit them. From these visits resulted wishes and requests to be instructed in the Catholic religion and received into the Church. This aroused the displeasure and opposition of the preachers, of whom there were several in the neighborhood.

REV. TIM REEVES.

The preachers began to hold meetings and revivals near the Catholic settlement, and in those places where the parties lived who were known to be inclining towards the Catholic Church. At one of these meetings, a preacher named Tim Reeves, who was afterwards a notorious guerilla leader during the war, delivered the following discourse, aimed directly at some persons before him, who were then preparing for baptism in the Catholic Church, and who reported his words to me. "Wait," said he, "until the Catholic Church gets hold on some of you, and then you will know what it is to be a Catholic. I was at Cape Girardeau a short time ago. There is a big Catholic church at Cape Girardeau, and the place is full of Romanists. I went to the church and stood near the door to see what was going on. The old priest had an image, which he held up in his hands, for the people to adore. The old priest had it so fixed on wires, that whatever he said, the image would say it after him. Then the people threw themselves down on their faces, and gave the old priest lots of money. Do you want to belong to that old priest, and to the idolatrous Church of Rome, that makes the people adore images in order to cheat them out of their money?" The persons who reported this sermon of Tim Reeves to me, were shocked by the accusations he made against the Catholic Church, which they protested they could not believe from him, and that he must have wilfully prevaricated. I apologized for Tim Reeves, that possibly he may have been in good faith, not knowing the ceremonies of the Catholic Church or their meaning. I explained, that on Good Friday, the day on which our Blessed Lord died for us on the Cross, the Catholic Church commemorated that sacred event by causing to be exposed and held up before the people, a large cross, with the image of Christ crucified upon it. The priest who held up the cross in his arms, said, to the people present, in Latin: "Behold the wood of the Cross, upon which hung the Savior of the world; let us come and adore." Then the deacon, standing near the priest, repeated the same words, in the name of the congregation present. "Behold the wood of the Cross, upon which hung the Savior of the world; come let us adore." It was this answering of the deacon to the priest, that made poor ignorant Tim Reeves believe that it was the image that spoke. That is all that poor ignorant Tim Reeves, preacher as he is, knows about the subject. He was likewise in ignorance when he said that the money collected was for the priest. The priest very likely may have collected the money, but it was not for himself, but for the Holy Sepulchre of our Lord, and for other such holy places in Jerusalem, that needed to be sacredly guarded and kept in repair; the offerings of the people in our churches on Good Friday, going to this truly sacred purpose. What seemed strange, ridiculous, and wicked, to Tim Reeves, was no doubt very pious and praiseworthy to Catholics. But it would be useless to explain this to such men as he, who can see nothing but malice and wickedness in Catholics and in the Catholic Church.

ANOTHER REVEREND.

There was another preacher there, a circuit rider, who, it was said, set himself up to great advantage as an opponent of the Catholic Church. "Priest Hogan," said he, "sent for me, and offered me a large salary to teach school in his settlement. I was about to accept the offer, but when he proposed that I should teach the Romanist catechism, I said no, that I would not teach that wicked catechism were I to get the whole world." Priest Hogan avers that he never saw or spoke to such person that he knows of or can remember.

A SICK CALL.

In answer to a sick call from a member of a family living on Mill Creek in Ripley county, at a place about one mile north of the Arkansas line and about thirteen miles south from the settlement chapel, I set out on horseback, taking with me the Holy Oils and the Most Blessed Sacrament. It was usual with me, when apprehensive of danger on my journeys through the woods, to carry suspended by a string from the pommel of the saddle, a sword cane, which, when at home, I hung on a nail in the log wall of my house. On setting out on this occasion I took the cane with me and suspended it from the saddle. Afterwards, as I proceeded, when at about a quarter of a mile distance from my house, I felt very much dissatisfied with myself, and was even shocked to think that I should have with me, for my protection, so murderous a weapon, when I should rather depend, and entirely so, on the Real Divine Presence with me when on an errand of mercy. I knew not how or why I felt so fully persuaded. I returned to the house, dismounted from the saddle, put the sword cane back in its place, and resumed my journey.

THE DIVINE PROTECTION.

My way was towards the south-east, along Mill Creek. When passing by the residence of Judge Hutcheson on said creek, about three miles from where the sick person lived, the judge went out to meet me and invited me into his house. I told him of the errand on which I was journeying, and that it was not customary on such duty to delay on the way. But I said to him, that on my return the next day, I would with great pleasure pay him a visit. Accordingly on the next day, as I was returning, I called at the judge's house and inquired for him. I was told he was with his men, who were harvesting wheat in a field near by along the roadside. I rode on towards the harvest field, and when near the men harvesting, I asked where the judge was or could be found. They replied that he had been with them a few minutes before, and had then just left to go to another part of the farm. At that moment, one of the workmen, a gigantic, active young man, stepping aside from the others and walking towards me, requested me to speak with him, that he had something private and important to say to me. I waited for him. He bounded over the fence into the road. We proceeded some distance together; he on foot, I on horseback. Soon the road diverged from the farm into the woods. I said, "Now sir, we are alone, let me hear what you have to say; perhaps there is something you wish that I can do for you." He looked at me and around, and said: "Not yet, let us walk on a little farther." We walked on and were soon quite into the woods, out of seeing and hearing of every one. Apprehensive of danger, I stopped my horse, and said again, "Now sir, let me hear what you wish to say to me." He at once darted for and grabbed my horse's bridle. I as quickly dismounted and stood near him, holding the bridle rein in my hand. He eyed me fiercely with the look of a murderer; and that instant, seizing me in his powerful hands, insulted me past all endurance by acts that were disgustingly vile and shockingly brutal. It was the moment to use the sword cane, but I thank God that I had not it. He raised his hand to strike me, but before the blow fell, there was a shriek or a scream; it came from Judge Hutcheson, who was in time to save me from direst harm.

PULPIT AND PENITENTIARY.

On the next day, Judge Hutcheson asked me to prosecute the aggressor, against whom there was evidence that he had engaged to provoke me to anger by insult, and then to kill me as would appear in self-defense. Others said also that the testimony to be produced would implicate an ex-preacher as an accessory. The judge said, moreover, that my assailant was a noted criminal who had already served a term in the Arkansas penitentiary. I replied to the judge, thanking him sincerely for his protection and interference in my behalf, and for his kind offer to befriend me and to do me justice. "As regards my assailant," said I, "I forgive him from my heart, and I pray God to forgive him and mend him. It is all over now. I wish that unfortunate fellow no harm."

CHAPTER X.

OLD FRIENDS CRYING FOR HELP.

WHILE these things were going on in the settlement in southern Missouri, I received many letters from those I had left behind me in northern Missouri, complaining that they had not heard Mass or received the Sacraments since I left them, that many had died without the last Sacraments, and that then presently there were many children unbaptized and many sick needing to be prepared for death. I told them to call on Reverend Father Scanlon of St. Joseph, and Reverend Father Murphy of Hannibal to attend them, especially in sickness. They replied that they had done so, but that these priests could not undertake to leave their own congregations and go on long journeys to others not of their charge, and who should have a priest themselves. I then again laid the wants and complaints of these Catholics of the interior of northwest Missouri before His Grace the Archbishop of St. Louis, who replied as before, that he had no priest to spare to send them, and that he did not know of any priest willing to resign his place. Some time afterwards, however, he informed me that two of the Lazarist Fathers of Cape Girardeau, had promised him, at his request, to go for that one time on a missionary visit to those in whose behalf I had written to him. Accordingly, Rev. T. D. O'Keeffe and Rev. P. McMennamy did set out from Cape Girardeau or the Barrens, and did make a missionary tour through those places where as I had stated, Catholics lived, without having a priest to attend them. Soon again however, the same complaints began to be made as before, and in addition thereto, there was another matter requiring attention.

A NEW DIFFICULTY.

The saw-mill owners who furnished lumber for building the church at Chillicothe, put in an additional bill, not before heard of, amounting to about seventy-five dollars, which they said they had previously presented, but that it remained unpaid. It was in vain that I wrote to the aforesaid Reverend Fathers at St. Joseph and Hannibal, and to the Catholics who had settled at or near Chillicothe, to make a collection and pay the debt. All that I had applied to, had affairs of their own to mind, and could not therefore attend to my affairs, as they regarded the church business at Chillicothe. Besides, as some of them said, it was to no purpose to make such collection and payment, since, as every one saw, the church at Chillicothe was given up and abandoned. Why, therefore, think of relieving it of debt? To make matters worse, the creditors entered suit and served me with notice thereof. Putting my affairs at the

settlement in some order for the time being, I set out
for North Missouri, uncertain how long or short my
absence might be. The intervening journey had
however, in the course of the year just elapsed, become much easier. After a ride on horseback of
about one hundred miles from the settlement to the
Pilot Knob; the rest of the way, over railroads lately
completed, was easy enough. I soon reached Chillicothe, the end of my journey. This was in the last
days of October, 1859.

THE DIFFICULTY REMOVED.

Arrived at Chillicothe, I was received with joy.
And it did not take me long to collect the money to
pay the saw-mill debt. During the month of November I visited the incipient missions, east and west,
and all around, wherever I had heard of Catholics
having settled. The joy of having Mass again, caused
them to entreat me to stay with them. I expressed
the great pleasure it would give me to serve them,
but I made them no binding promise.

SOUTHWARD ONCE MORE.

I set out again for southern Missouri where I
stayed the greater part of December, attending,
among other duties, to the instruction of some
converts heretofore partly prepared and now baptized and received into the Church. My recent visit
to North Missouri impressed me with the idea that
the increasing number of Catholics there, could not
be neglected, much less totally abandoned. The

time too seemed ripe for building more churches in northern Missouri. The children there needed to be instructed for First Communion and Confirmation, and the church at Chillicothe was yet without the sacred rite of dedication.

AGAIN NORTHWARD AND OUT OF SEASON.

For these purposes, and for such time, longer or shorter, as it would take me to accomplish them, I was again northward bound. Unlike the happy little birds of spring and autumn, ever hying their way in season to more genial climes, it was my untoward fate, poor bird of passage that I was, to face northward, and out of season, against cold wintry blasts. The last days of December, 1859, found me again in Chillicothe, meditating much work to do.

CHAPTER XI.

TWO years and a half before, when setting out from St. Louis, the railroads in course of construction from that city into the interior of the State, had been completed to the following places, namely: the North Missouri to Warrenton, the Iron Mountain to Hopewell, the Hannibal and St. Joseph to Shelbina, and the Missouri Pacific to Jefferson City. With the exception of these short distances, journeys in Missouri were made by steamboat, stage, or on horseback. Travelling by steamboat was pleasant, but practicable only along the large rivers. Inland travel afforded much rougher experience. East and west throughout North Missouri, between Hannibal and St. Joseph, a distance of two hundred miles, there was daily, each way, a line of four-horse stage coaches, carrying passengers, mail, and express. The schedule time from Hannibal to St. Joseph, or vice versa, was forty eight hours, continuous travelling. The stage fare was sixteen dollars, and refreshments during the journey cost about four dollars additional. The incessant jolting and shaking, cramped in a close vehicle amongst a crowd of weary passengers, without sleep or rest, to say nothing of the parching heat in summer and the freezing cold in winter, was as much as the stoutest could endure. And there were, besides, many dangers, disappointments, and delays that were not on the schedule. In the spring rains and ice thaws, travelling by stage was necessarily suspended; the prairie mire being for road purposes practically bottomless.   More dangerous still were the midsummer deluges that swept away bridges and culverts and flooded the low lands, to the dismay of stage coach travellers.

WATERLOGGED.

On a summer's night in 1858, travelling westward through Linn and Livingston counties in a four horse mail stage crowded with passengers, and in care of a driver unacquainted with, and then on his first trip over the road, the horses rushed over a bridge spanning Medicine River, and thence onward unchecked to the low land on the west side, which for miles across and up and down stream, was covered like the sea with water from a recent cloud burst. The horses at once got terrified and unmanageable, and floundered about in the water, kicking and pulling and jerking against each other.   Soon the horses and stage came to a standstill, the water being up to the horses' sides, and rising.   The passengers became greatly alarmed, and the more so as being strangers and unacquainted with the place, they thought every moment they were about to sink to rise no more. The driver, the most terrified of all, was literally at sea, having lost his presence of mind as well as his reckoning. Dark night brooded over the scene which was but sky and water everywhere around; nor was there a friendly light house on the distant shore to cheer with its silver rays the trackless water's wide expanse.

THE RESCUE.

Fortunately there was one aboard the stage, who though not to the manner born in North Missouri, had been there for some time of late, and had taken observations in passing through the country. Electing himself captain of the drowning stage, he gave his orders as follows. Driver, down with you from that seat, into the water. Unhitch your wheel horses and halter them to the body of the stage. Next, unhitch your leaders. Mount one of them while I mount the other. Passengers, be not afraid, I know your danger and shall soon get help to rescue you. Driver, follow me, I know the way. On we went, wading through the water in single file, towards a farm house on the highlands, about two miles distant. We got there, not varying a point from our course. Good farmer, said I, I do not know your name, but I know you are a good man. We are in great distress. The west-bound stage, full of passengers, is stuck fast, water-logged in Medicine Swamp. The horses balked and kicked in the water and would go no farther. But the water is not yet too deep. Have you any oxen here, trained to work?

Oh yes, he said, I understand you, I know what you want. Boys, my sons, get the oxen, get the best of them, yoke up Buck and Bright and Berry and Brandy. Take a log chain with you. Get on the backs of the oxen. Follow these men through the water. When you get to the stage, hitch on to it, and haul it out to dry land. Arrived at the stage, Buck and Bright were soon in tug as wheel horses, and Berry and Brandy as leaders. The ox whip cracked, the stage heaved to, on it went. One strong pull, a pull together, never stopping until the stage was on dry land. On calling the roll of passengers it was found that, although none of them had drowned or died of fright, most of them were much injured by bites of mosquitoes; the ladies, as usual in such cases, having suffered most. In a few minutes a liberal purse was made up for the daring ox drivers. The horses, once more in harness and on solid ground, were bounding forward to make up lost time. Six miles farther on, at Chillicothe, the captain of the water-logged stage, alighting therefrom, bid adieu to his companions of the journey, not one of them, so far as he knows, having heard his name or learned who or whence he was. It was fortunate for them that he had lately learned how to yoke and drive oxen in a certain new settlement in Southern Missouri.

ROCKS AND SHOALS.

Traveling in Southern Missouri was even more difficult than in Northern Missouri, and was for the most part possible only on horseback, on account of the ruggedness of the country and the rockiness of the roads. The rivers, being shallow and hard-bed-ded, did not require bridges, as fords were numerous and good. Occasionally, in heavy rains, the rivers rose quickly past fording; but as they subsided as quickly, the delay to let the high water run by was not long. The difficulties arose mostly from the long distances to be traversed along trackless divides or over deep valleys and steep hill-sides through the forests.

WEATHERING A GALE.

Once, being somewhat in a hurry and anxious to make the shortest way over the hills and through the forests, I was speeding along pleasantly on horse-back, guiding my course by the direction of the sun. Soon the sky became overcast, and more so as the thickening shades of evening came on apace. No longer able to steer my course from the direction of the sun, I made good use of a large pocket com-pass I carried with me. After nightfall, I could still use the compass by the aid of a match light. The match light however soon failed me, as the over-cast clouds brought on gusts of wind and pelting rain that blew out the light. There was yet a resource—to hold the compass open and read it by the flashes of lightning that darted across the horizon. This, too, soon failed. The compass exposed so often to the wind and rain lost the light silver wire that was tied on the magnetized arm of the needle, so that now, both arms of the needle being alike and indistinguishable, there was no longer a possibility of determining north or south, or any cardinal point. Like a ship in a gale, unable to make headway, I was obliged to heave to, and wait for clearer skies.

THE WILDNESS OF YOUTH.

And here I may apologize for having given myself, unnecessarily as may have been, to enterprises of responsibility, hardship and danger, no doubt regarded by wiser heads than mine as but the wildness of youth. What I have to say for myself is stated cumulatively in what I have hereinbefore said on the abnormal condition of catholic emigrants in Missouri and on the remedy to better that condition. If I would advance some of many other reasons, they would be the following. In early boyhood I took great delight reading in the Annals of the Society for the Propagation of the Faith, the achievements of Missionary Priests in far off countries, braving all obstacles to convert benighted nations to the light of Christianity. I followed these Holy Missionaries in spirit and with all the ardor of my soul into China, Japan, Borneo, Siam, Tongking, and other equally remote or unknown regions of the world. But nowhere did their lives and labors seem so grand and heroic to me as on the Great Plains of North America, along the sources and banks of the world famed rivers, the Missouri and the Mississipi and their numerous tributaries—a country which they enrapturously described as of surpassing beauty, as fresh as if new made from the hand of the Creator, and inhabited only by wild men, who shared their illimitable solitude with countless wild animals, which they pursued with all the ardor of the chase over grassy hunting grounds.

GOD'S UNSEARCHABLE WAYS.

It was also my good fortune in early boyhood to have had placed in my hands by dear friends interested in my education, the several successive annual issues of the American Catholic Almanac, which I scanned with delight from page to page, dwelling especially on the gracefulness and beauty of the several engraved cathedrals that frontispieced the respective diocesan descriptions. Amongst these there was one, that of St. Louis, with its lofty cross-crowned spire piercing the skies, that I found myself most constantly looking at, and that above all won my admiration. But how could I know then what the wonderful ways of God have since so happily brought to pass; that in the far off Western Hemisphere and within that cathedral I was to receive ordination as Priest, and from the consecrated hands of the Venerable Archbishop, whose jurisdiction grasped the whole extent of those boundless and beautiful missionary fields, contemplating which my youthful mind grew fascinated in wonder.

CHAPTER XII.

AT the time that I entered upon the duties of the mission in North Missouri, that is to say in the month of September, 1857, there were in that part of the interior of the State thirty-two counties in a contiguous body of land, perhaps the finest in the world, having an area of sixteen thousand square miles, being once and a half as large as Belgium or half as large as Ireland, without a Catholic church or priest, and having exclusive of transient railroad laborers, not more than a dozen resident catholic families. Two years and a half later, that is to say at the beginning of 1860, with railroads completed from St. Louis to Hudson, which is now called Macon City, and from Hannibal to St. Joseph, and centrally traversing this great district, I set about making such missionary arrangements as might be satisfactory to Catholics intending to settle in it. For this purpose I thought best to name four principal places, at each which to say Mass once a month on a stated Sunday; and likewise to name about a dozen less important places, at each of which, if but even one catholic family would be found there, to say Mass once every three months, on the fifth Sunday occuring in certain months, or otherwise on holidays or week days. To bring this arrangement within the reach of Catholics wherever residing throughout the mission, and that they be informed of where I could be found at any and all times in case of sickness or other emergency, I issued the following missionary time table and distributed it as I went along, thereby keeping every member of my scattered flock in communication with me by telegraph or mail. My plan served my purpose admirably. A copy of the missionary time table in every catholic family gave information of the priest's movements at all times, and served as a monitory to Catholics to prepare for Mass and the reception of the sacraments, at the appointed times and places which were rigidly fixed and steadfastly kept.

MISSIONARY TIME TABLE.

On days not herein stated, and excepting railroad schedule time for traveling to and from places herein mentioned, the Priest may be found at his place of residence, Chillicothe.	APPOINTMENTS FOR —MASS— 1860.	Chillicothe	Macon City	Brookfield	Mexico	Cameron
	January - -	1	8	15	22	29
	February - -	5	12	19	26	
	March - -	4	11	18	25	
	April - - -	1	8	15	22	29
	May - - -	6	13	20	27	
	June - - -	3	10	17	24	
	July - - -	1	8	15	22	29
	August - - -	5	12	19	26	
	September -	2	9	16	23	30
	October - -	7	14	21	28	
	November - -	4	11	18	25	
	December - -	2	9	16	23	30
	Appointments for Mass on holidays and week days will be otherwise made and communicated.	1st Sunday	2nd Sunday	3rd Sunday	4th Sunday	5th Sunday

RAILROAD AND TELEGRAPH FREE.

To follow this time table, and with occasional changes it was strictly followed for several years, the average annual travelling including also journeys on sick calls, was about ten thousand miles, which at the railroad rates of fare then current, would cost about four hundred dollars per annum. The Railroad Presidents apprised by me of my total inability to pay this expense, with very great kindness and consideration as well as liberality, ordered me carried free of cost everywhere over their lines. The Subordinate Railroad officers, in a like spirit of liberality and kindness, and with a view to amplify favors, usually stopped their trains for me to get on and off even between stations. Many a time my heart more than my lips spoke a grateful "God bless you" to some poor brakeman or conductor, who more in need of rest himself than I, folded his overcoat or his blanket and put it softly under my head to rest me as I lay on the hard board seat in the caboose car, overcome by fatigue of several days and nights of labor and travel in succession. And how can I ever forget all these acts of kindness? Or how can I repay them? To mention each benefactor would be to name every brother railroad man, as I may call them, with whom I travelled. Honorable Isaac H. Sturgeon, of St. Louis, my life-long friend, President of the North Missouri Railroad in its early days, when it needed a man of enterprise, executive ability and influence to give it success, was always my kind, appreciative and encouraging benefactor. So also was the fearless, progressive and loyal New Englander J. T. K. Hayward, Esquire, President of the Hannibal & St. Joseph Railroad, my constant and worthy friend. And not by any means last, but rather among the first, best and noblest of all my friends was George H. Nettleton, Esquire, a gentleman beloved by everyone, who has done honor and given success to the many railroad enterprises that he has been in charge of. The telegraph lines, too, were placed at my disposal, free of cost, for all messages to or from me on missionary business. By these acts of continued liberality and kindness I was enabled to proceed with my work. Otherwise, want of travelling expenses, which the mission could by no means afford, would have put me to defeat, and driven me into obscurity.

ASCENSION THURSDAY, 1860.

Among the purposes that I set before me at the beginning of 1860, the Sacraments of Confirmation, and the dedication of the church at Chillicothe, were of first importance. In preparation for these events, catechism classes were taught Sunday after Sunday for several months at each mission station. The time set for First Communion and Confirmation was the Feast of the Ascension of our Lord, May 17, on which day, also, the church was to be dedicated. The railroad officers, with their usual generosity, gave a rate of travelling for the occasion at a mere nominal sum, so that parents as well as children could attend from all parts of the mission. The Right Reverend James Michael O'Gorman, D. D., Bishop of Raphanea, Vicar Apostolic of Nebraska, residing at Omaha, at the request of His Grace the Most Reverend Peter Richard Kenrick, Archbishop of St. Louis, administered Confirmation, dedicated the church, and preached on the occasion. Mass was celebrated by the Reverend Thomas Scanlon, rector of St. Joseph's Church, St. Joseph, Missouri. In the evening a sermon was preached by the Reverend James Murphy, rector of the Catholic Church at Hannibal. Afterwards Benediction of the Most Blessed Sacrament was given. Then all set out for their homes. The following are the names of those confirmed on that happy first occasion, ever memorable in the history of the Church in the interior of North Missouri.

TEMPLES OF THE LIVING GOD.

Catherine Ward,	John Ryan,
Anne Holland,	John McDonnell,
Andrew Lyons,	Daniel Graney,
Thomas Fitzpatrick,	Martin Rafter,
Michael Murray,	Michael Cotter,
Anne Bridget Murray,	Michael Sullivan,
Michael Murtagh,	John Cain,
Mary Murtagh,	Patrick Carney,
Anne Murtagh,	Michael Bowe,
Peter Murtagh,	Peter Quinn,

86

Marcella Murtagh, Margaret Kenny,
Mary Carter, Maria Donnelly,
Bridget Carter, Mary Kennedy,
Mary Cain, Anthony Mahon,
Patrick Keating, John Behan,
Ellen Walsh, John Dunn,
Jane M. A. Brown, Thomas Farrell,
Michael Dowd, Joseph T. Brown,
Catherine Arbuckles, John T. Brown,
Elizabeth Bruce, William P. Farrell,
Amanda Ryan, John Quealy,
Emilia Montague, John Toole,
Amanda Montague, Anthony Walsh.

BANCROFT.

The dedication of the church and the confirmation of the children being over, I turned my attention to other matters. Going northward on horseback a day's journey of forty miles, I found at a new place called Bancroft, in Davies County, a family lately settled there, comprising father, mother and their several grown up children, sons and daughters, all good Catholics. They were glad to see me, and to have Mass in their house, which was a neat but solitary cottage, far out on the broad, grassy, wind-swept prairie. They prepared themselves by prayer and confession, and with great piety assisted at Mass and received Holy Communion. The worthy Christian father, with very edifying humility, addressed me as follows as I was about to begin Mass. "Revcrend Father, it is so long since we heard Mass that we do not know when to kneel or when to stand. If you please, tell us what to do, so that we may hear Mass reverently as we ought."

BETHANY.

At Bethany, about sixteen miles northwest from Bancroft, I found a few Catholic families, who having wandered away several years before from some frontier catholic settlement in Kentucky, had almost entirely forgotton their religion; and the more so as the society in which they lived was pervaded by deep prejudice to the Catholic Church. I said Mass for them, at which only some of them assisted. My words and prayers were not wanting to incline them again towards the true mother Church and its saving and consoling duties as their only sure way to heaven.

EAGLEVILLE.

Near Eagleville, which is sixteen miles north of Bethany, I said Mass for some Catholics then settling there, who, like those at Bethany, having strayed far away, had grown almost indifferent to their religious duties, though retaining a reverential regard for their Mother the Church.

HICKORY BRANCH.

Turning homeward from Harrison County, Missouri, on the confines of Iowa, I reached Chillicothe in two day's journey. Setting out soon again, and as before on horseback, I travelled southeastward in-

to Chariton County, where at a place called Hickory
Branch, on the divide between the tributaries of the
Chariton and Grand Rivers, I found a catholic Ger-
man family of sincere piety and truly ardent zeal. I
stayed at their house and said Mass for them. They
were glad even to tears of joy to receive me. And
they begged of me to return to them again, and not
to abandon them, as they did not know where a
priest was to be found in the whole country around
them. Their fervent faith and warm generous piety
gave promise that God would bless the place they
had selected for their home, and that religion would
flourish therein.

BROOKFIELD.

Center Point, on the Hannibal and St. Joseph
Railroad, at which I had intended to build the first
church, having failed to become a place of importance
as it promised, gradually yielded its central destiny
to another town laid out some years later and several
miles farther westward, called Brookfield. I said
Mass for the first time at Brookfield on Dec. 20, 1859,
at the residence of Mr. Patrick Landrigan. Thenceforward, Mass was celebrated regularly there every
month, sometimes at the residence of Mr. James
Tooey, and sometimes at the residence of Mr. Michael
McGowan. The church at Brookfield owes much to
the generosity and zeal of Mr. James Tooey and his
brother Mr. Patrick Tooey and their families and
friends. James and Patrick Tooey were railroad

contractors who settled respectively at Brookfield and Thayer when their railroad work was done. Thayer, like Center Point which it adjoined, was an ambitious and unsuccessful aspirant for the honors of the great central town that was expected to grow up in the interior of northwest Missouri. Patrick Tooey invested and lost the greater part of his honest and hard-earned money in this phantom town, to which he gave the name of a wealthy and influential stockholder in the railroad, who notwithstanding the compliment paid him, did not favor the project that bore his name. Mr. Tooey erected a fine mansion there with many adjoining outbuildings, which he soon lost by fire, and without insurance. His pious venerable mother died there. There also his devoted saintly wife departed from him to a better world. At this lady's funeral a touching incident occurred that brought tears to the eyes of every one present. As she lay in state in her funeral robes awaiting burial, her youngest child, about two years old, approached the catafalque and calling his mamma offered her some candy he held in his hand. Not getting an answer from his mamma, he climbed up to her side, and putting the candy between her lips pressed her to eat it. Poor child! you did not know then what you learned afterwards, that it was a sore calamity for you to lose your good fond mother. Both ladies, mother and daughter as they were in affection, lie buried side by side. Their resting place is in a secluded little cemetery near by, the first set apart in that neighborhood for catholic burial, in a grove on the brow of a hill on the verge of a prairie. God rest their souls and the souls of all the faithful departed.

James Tooey settled with his good christian wife and family at Brookfield. He prospered there, merchandising in town and owning cultivated lands in the suburbs. Mrs. McGowan, wife of Michael McGowan at whose house I frequently said Mass in Brookfield before the church was built there, is the worthy sister of James and Patrick Tooey. The church at Brookfield was begun early in 1860, and having progressed rapidly and without mishap, was dedicated in August that year.

MACON CITY.

Soon after the dedication of the church at Brookfield, the little church built then or soon afterwards at Macon City, was blessed and opened to the Catholic people settling there and fast growing into a congregation. The mission at Indian Creek in Monroe county, being at this time (1860) without a priest, I was called there frequently to attend the sick and administer the sacraments. On one such visit I remained there eight days, from the 19th to the 25th of March, saying Mass daily, preaching, baptizing and hearing confessions.

THE SAVAGE RUSSIANS.

In the summer of 1860, happening to be at Macon

City, my attention was aroused by a hubbub at the
railway depot. Curious to know what it was about,
I hastened to the spot. The North Missouri train
from St. Louis had arrived, and its passengers with
their baggage had been transferred to the corresponding west-bound Hannibal and St. Joseph train, standing on the track, awaiting the signal for departure. I
noticed that along the side of this waiting train, for its
whole length, a row of heads had been thrust out
through the windows, and with open ears listening
to the racket that was going on. On the platform
of the railway depot there was also a curious
crowd of gazers gathered around a pile of trunks
of rough foreign manufacture of untanned cow-
hide. On one side of the pile stood a band of
foreigners, mostly young or middle-aged men,
dressed in black or blue blouses, and wearing tight
fitting traveling caps. On the opposite side stood an
excited red haired young man, talking loud and making
forcible gestures at the foreigners.

Recognizing the boisterous auburn haired gentleman as my worthy good hearted friend, Mr. Sleeper
the station agent and telegraph operator, I said to him:
"Ho Mr. Sleeper, what's the matter with you?"
"What's the matter with me," he replied, "why there
is a pack of savage Russians here. Every man of them
has a half dozen trunks. Look at the horrid pile.
Why, they are a car load. And these fellows
wont pay a red cent extra baggage for them.

They can't understand me, and I can't understand their jabber, and I don't know what to do." Noticing that some of the savage Russians were speaking among themselves, I listened to them awhile, and soon discovered that I could solve the problem. The language they spoke was not Russian, but French. I soon learned their story. They apologized for their neglected begrimed appearance, saying that they were after a long and rough voyage from Havre to New York, and that since they had left New York, being already several days and nights on the road, they had no opportunity to make themselves properly presentable. Furthermore, they said that their journey had cost them more than they had anticipated, and as missionaries they had thought that their baggage, which contained only books, vestments and clothing, would not be charged for. Turning to Mr. Sleeper I said: "Ah, Sleeper, you are certainly mistaken. These men are not Savage Russians, as you say. They are French priests and students going out as missionaries to the Indians. Their sooty, dust-stained condition is unavoidable. Their long rough sea voyage to New York and their hard experience on the cars night and day from New York here, has put them in the condition you see. They have nothing in these trunks but some vestments and books for their chapels and schools. You wouldn't charge these poor missionaries, would you?" "Are they really missionaries?" said he. "Yes," said I. "All right," said he, "tell them to go aboard." Then with his own hands he helped the train men to load the trunks in the baggage car. He waved his hand, the engine bell rang, the whistle blew, and the train was away.

MACON CITY AGAIN.

Among the devoutest worshippers in the Catholic church at Macon City, built, as already stated, in 1860, was Miss Mary Hall of Randolph county, sister of Judge William A. Hall and of Governor Willard P. Hall. She was usually the first in church on Sunday morning. Having arranged the altar with flowers and flower vases, and with altar linens and altar lights—her own gifts; she then devoted herself to prayer, confession, Mass, and Holy Communion. Afterwards, when leaving the church, her heart seemed to linger there, so earnestly did she look back to the sacred place; her face modestly veiled, and scant notice taken of any one, the while. Those who knew her were not surprised, when they heard that she had entered a convent of the Sisters of Mercy; where, wearing the Holy Religious Habit, she lived and died, a saint.

During the war, soon following, the Macon City church was often occupied by soldiers. In 1864, when Macon City was threatened by the rebels at Glascow, the church was gutted and almost demolished; its pews, altar, and floors, having been taken to camp for fuel, or piled into the ramparts for defense.

CHAPTER XIII.

WAR'S ALARMS.

EIGHTEEN hundred and sixty from beginning to end was a year of tremendous excitement and inauspicious portent. Four great national parties, having their respective political platforms and chosen leaders, entered the arena contending for dominancy. But one party could be victorious. The vanquished, or those who so considered themselves, rushed on to the bad principle of national disruption. The party elected to office aligned itself, as in duty bound, to defend national unity. Peace proposals were flung to the winds. The sword was drawn to decide the issue. Thirty millions of people begirding themselves with deadly weapons and falling into antagonistic battle lines, their hearts filled with hatred of each other, was a scene that can never be witnessed again until the world's final tribulation has come. Property became at once of no value. Home afforded no shelter. Friendship, and even the closest family ties, fell off into party lines. Churches and schools, religious and benevolent associations, public works and private enterprises, were suddenly suspended or paralyzed. All that was, was comprehended in one word—war. The tread and tramp of armies on foot and on horseback, the clatter of cannon wheels and the clanking of weapons, the hoarse commands of military men marshaling their forces, made a constant din and a never-ending pageant. Soon, with appalling force, the two tidal waves of wrath and power fell upon each other. Out from their recoil came the shouts of victory and the moans of defeat; and, with both, the wails and cries of widows and orphans, to whom the strife, end as it may, could bring no hope or comfort. The peacefully inclined fled in terror whithersoever they could, to places of safety—to the Pacific shores, to the Canada borders, to countries beyond the sea.

WAR'S DEVASTATIONS.

Missouri as a Border State, and consequently as a battle ground, lost its tens of thousands—fully as many by flight as by combat. My poor settlements suffered irretrievably. The one in Southern Missouri especially became broken and scattered; all who could, having fled therefrom. Ripley County, in which my Southern Settlement was principally located, suffered more than any other part of the State. Campbell's Gazetter of Missouri, in a few words, records its sad fate. "The County suffered severely during the Civil War, being occupied alternately by both armies, besides being invaded by marauding parties and bushwhackers, who murdered peaceful citizens, and destroyed houses, fences, and crops, until towards the close of the war scarcely a

male citizen was permitted to remain at home, un-
molested. The County Seat was first pillaged and
then burned, only two or three houses of the entire
town being saved." From cavalry soldiers on duty in
that county I learned, that corn to feed their horses had
to be carried by them in sacks behind them on their
horse's backs a distance of eighty miles; not so much
as an ear of corn being left, that they could find, in
that whole country. Alas! the devastations of war
and the woes and sorrows that follow after it. Who
now will build up those waste places? Who now
will lead back the poor scattered settlers to their
humble but ruined homes? Who now will rekindle
for them the light of faith or preach the word of God
to them in their little chapel beneath the pines in the
forest? Has all that was done and endured there,
been for nothing? Is there no hope for a place once
so dear and so sacred? To the most adorable will of
God, whose ways are ever full of mercy and above
our understanding, we most profoundly bow.

THE RUGGED ISSUE.

The opening days of 1861 were not hopeful of
peace or harmony for Missouri, and were therefore
unfavorable to my missionary work. On the 3rd of
January, 1861, Governor Stewart, in his valedictory
on the momentous conflict impending, expressed the
hope that Missouri would "hold to the union" undeterred by North or South. On the same day Governor Jackson, in his inaugural message, outlined the

duty of Missouri to be, "to stand by the South. "To carry out this policy he thought the best way would be to call a State Convention. Pursuantly, the General Assembly on the 18th of January passed a bill calling an election, to be held on the 18th of February, to choose delegates to a State Convention, to consider the relations of the State of Missouri to the United States and to the several states. At the appointed time, the 28th of February, the Convention met, and resolved, that Missouri had no cause for secession; and that Missouri's duty was, to promote peace and harmony, so far as possible by legislative efforts.

STANDING BY THE SOUTH.

On the 18th of January, in the moments after the passage of the bill calling the State Convention, Governor Jackson introduced by message to the General Assembly, the Hon. Daniel Russell, Commissioner from the State of Mississippi, to the people of Missouri, to tell them that they were expected to co-operate with the south in its efficient measures for safety and defence. The efficient measures of the South, taken or intended to be taken for safety and defence, were the following, as of fact and date: 1860, Dec. 10, South Carolina's United States Senators withdrew from Congress; Dec. 12, South Carolina seized the United States forts Moultrie and Pinkney; Dec. 14, South Carolina's United States Representatives withdrew from Congress; Dec. 21, South Carolina seceded from the United States; Dec.

24, Georgia seized the United States Arsenal at Augusta; 1861, Jan. 3, Georgia seized the United States forts Pulaski and Jackson; Jan. 9, South Carolina fired on the United States steamer Star of the West; Jan. 10, Florida seceded from the United States; Jan. 11, Alabama seceded from the United States; Jan. 16, Georgia seceded from the United States; Jan. 26, Louisiana seceded from the United States; Jan. —, Mississippi seceded from the United States; Jan. —, Louisiana seized the United States forts Jackson and St. Philip; Jan. —, Louisiana seized the United States Arsenal at Baton Rouge; Jan. 31, Louisiana seized the United States Custom House and Mint at New Orleans; April 12, South Carolina bombarded the United States fort Sumpter; April 17, Governor Jackson of Missouri refused to help to maintain the Union or to recover its forts and arsenals; April 20, Governor Jackson of Missouri seized the United States arsenal at Liberty, Missouri, with its arms and ammunition; May 10, Governor Jackson's Brigadier General, commanding Missouri State Militia at Camp Jackson, St. Louis, declared that he had no intention against the United States, its property or representatives, which declaration, in the light of the foregoing facts, and especially of the last named fact, must have meant strategy; June 11, Governor Jackson, his State Officers and General Assembly, retired from the Missouri State Capitol and went South.

HOLDING TO THE UNION.

Missouri's latest elected representatives, the Delegates to the State Convention, called for the purpose of considering Missouri's interests in the secession crisis, decided, as we have already seen, that Missouri had no cause for secession, and that her duty was to remain firm in the Union. This policy was clearly indicated by the Convention at its opening, by its refusal to make official reply to Luther J. Glenn, Commissioner from the State of Georgia, to induce Missouri to secede. Commissioner Glenn's communications were laid on the table to die, and then solemnly pigeon-holed, to rise no more. The Convention still furthering its wise, firm and quiet course, declared the flight of Governor Jackson and his State Officers and General Assembly men from the State Capitol a "de facto" vacating of their respective offices, and proceeded forthwith to fill said vacancies by a provisional government in harmony with the interests of the state and the wishes of its people as expressed by their representatives. Thenceforward, though war went on, there was no dissension in Missouri's State Counsels. Missouri owes an everlasting debt of gratitude to her steady and wise statesmen, who safeguarded her destiny in that dark and tempestuous hour.

MOBILIZING FOR BATTLE.

The call of the President of the United States for men to maintain the Union and to recover its forts

and arsenals, though refused by the Missouri Rebel
Governor, was responded to nevertheless by the people
of Missouri, who were loyal to the Union, and who
formed themselves into military organizations in aid
of the United States. To the aid of these came the
regiments from Illinois, Iowa and Kansas, quickly
mustered into service in answer to the President's
call; their first duty being to maintain and keep open
the railways lately built through Northern Missouri,
and now used to convey Union troops to the front to
resist the rebellion onset. On the other hand, the
great body of Missourians who had resolved to stand
by the South, in obedience to calls for troops from
their leaders, Governor Jackson and General Price,
had likewise formed themselves into battalions and
regiments, their first assigned duty being to destroy
the lines of communication that the Union men had
aligned themselves to defend. Hence the first fierce
war struggles in North Missouri occured in my mission, along the lines of the Hannibal & St. Joseph
and the North Missouri Railways; the passing trains
being fired upon from every convenient ambush, and
the bridges and trestles being burnt and rebuilt many
times in succession. No one then travelling on these
railways could be sure of his life for one minute.
And many a life was lost by the flying bullets that
smashed and splintered through the cars, and by the
derailed trains hurled down over precipices and em-
bankments.

THE DEATHLY CHASM.

It shall always remain fresh in my grateful memory, that I am indebted to Almighty God's Infinite
Mercy for my safety in twenty-one railroad wrecks
of more or less destructiveness, through which I
passed in those times so wasteful of human life. Indeed it used to seem to me that death was very near
me, ever hovering at my back and shoulders. Such
feelings, however, did not give me much concern, as
I had learned through sense of duty to disregard
danger. The many railroad wrecks that occurred
were not all the direct result of battle. They were
oftener its indirect results. The railroads as property were worth nothing to their owners. Nor was
the future at all bright, that they ever would be of
any value to any one, so probable did it seem that
the war would destroy everything. Hence the value-
less railroads were suffered to go out of repair, and
to lapse into a most unserviceable condition. And if
any repairs at all were made it was usually under
military protection and for military purposes, and
the repairs made were very temporary. The railroads, because used for carrying Federal soldiers and
munitions of war, were hated and stormed at by
the other party as something wicked that should be
exterminated; and civilians and non-combatants, travelling over them, were in the same predicament as
the abhorred enemy, sought to be put out of existence. A notable example of this occurred almost at

the very outset of the war, at Platte River bridge, Buchanan County, where a train full of people were sent down to death through a dark chasm, in the night; all timely notice to the approaching train, of its danger, having been prevented by the men who destroyed the bridge, and then patrolled the neighborhood, waiting to see the inhuman results of their cold-blooded planning. I had travelled on that train that evening from Macon City to Chillicothe. At Chillicothe, as I was leaving the train, I could not but be apprehensive of danger to those aboard it, and having to journey farther. Being well acquainted with the conductor and brakemen in charge of the train, who were good, kind-hearted christian men, I asked them if they thought they could go through safe that night, to their journey's end. The conductor replied to me. "Oh, yes, sir, as we have travelled safe as far as Chillicothe, we consider the danger past. You need not be apprehensive for our safety for the rest of the way." The train passed out from the station, and was soon on its way, speeding out of sight. Three hours later, these two good men, conductor and brakeman, Stephen Cutler and John Fox, were forever at their journey's end, down in the bottom of the Platte, in the heap of the dead.

THE CHURCH MILITANT.

Happening to be in Brookfield for a day on some missionary duty, the railroad train dispatcher gave word in haste to the officer in command of a military detachment guarding the town, that telegraph communication had been cut off in all directions, and that likely some danger was impending. At once the drums beat tattoo to arms. The soldiers were soon in line. The commanding officer stood at their head. All eyes were turned on the surrounding hills, looking for the advance of battle. Just then messengers came running in haste, saying the rebels had burned the railroad bridges east and west, and were marching on Brookfield to take it. The tattoo beat again, this time through the streets, summoning all capable of bearing arms, to the military headquarters, to get muskets and accoutrements, to fall into line with the soldiers, for the common defence. Great was the confusion. "Hurrying to and fro, and arming in hot haste." Brookfield was an extra loyal town. Gaily and defiantly from every house-top, and from every balcony and airy window, the stars and stripes hung out, basking in the morning and evening sunshine, and fluttering in the prairie breezes. Union men from near and far, when riding by on the trains, never failed to take off their hats, and to hurrah for Brookfield and its ever floating stars and stripes. But it was holiday, not to say sham attire. Oh! the terror! the terror! the Rebels are coming; soon every flag in town was hauled down and hid away, not unlikely in the cellars. Truly, the dressy man on parade is not the bravest in battle. The only loyal flags that dared to float that day in Brookfield, "flinging out their folds to the battle and the breeze,"were the ones carried by the Color Sergeant's hands,and the one that floated from mast head at military headquarters. The central point for defence was the railroad station, the round house, the machine shops, and the long lines of freight cars standing on the tracks. Around these some slight breast works had been already thrown up, and some rifle pits dug here and there. Within these inclosures and fortifications,all men in town, civilians and soldiers, had hastened. Taking choice to be with the men, rather than among the women and children, I, too, stood within the entrenchments, expecting the onset, if not the issue of the impending battle. Standing up against the inside wall of the round house, were several rifles, with the military donnings belonging, waiting to be taken up by some improvised soldiers. I must confess that,in my horror and hatred of war,I became at that moment irrepressibly war-like—which was a paradox. Arraying myself in a somewhat military attire, I, too, in the impulse of the moment, rifle in hand, stood in with the Boys in Blue. My foolish episode gave rise to much merriment to my companions in arms, at the expense of a Preacher who stood by; and who, invited by them to "go and do likewise," sneaked away between the railroad engines,and hid himself in a corner of the round house. I make full confession of my utter discomfiture on that occasion, by my brother the Preacher, who was the better christian, and no doubt the wiser man for his personal safety. The enemy not appearing as was expected, it was resolved to reconnoitre for their whereabouts. For this purpose a masked battery on wheels was provided. Some railroad freight cars, bulwarked all round inside with rows of railroad ties breast high, and filled with soldiers, the muzzles of their guns run out through port holes in the car's sides, were sent out to patrol the road in both directions—east and west of Brookfield. After some hours the masked battery on wheels returned. The news it brought was, that Brush Creek bridge, sixteen miles east from Brookfield, and Parson Creek bridge, a like distance west from Brookfield, had been burned by bodies of rebel troops marching southward, and that said troops had already moved out of sight, and were far away. The military problem was then, but too late, easy of solution. The Rebel Soldiers, going south to join General Price, had no intention of attacking Brookfield. Their purpose, burning the bridges, was to prevent Brookfield following and attacking them, which was in Brookfield's power to do with much effect, if informed in time of their line of march, and if reinforced by troops from Stations east and west on the railroad. The information which the rebels feared, could not have been communicated, as the wires had been cut. Neither could the reinforcements be brought together in time, by railroad, two important bridges, thirty miles apart, having been destroyed. The Rebels were victors. They carried south a large body of recruits and many fine military horses, through the Federal lines, without losing a man or firing a shot.

ONE HUNDRED MILES OF FIRE.

Owing to the incapacity, and perplexity of plans and purposes, of the many Federal Generals set up and suspended in Missouri in 1861, the state was in the greatest confusion and uncertainty as to its future. The confusion was at its height, and was general throughout the state, after the Federal defeats at Wilson's Creek and Lexington. There seemed then no hope whatever of peace. And no one could forecast results. In order to be more centrally situated in my mission, and for the purpose of having shorter distances to travel, I changed my place of residence from Chillicothe to Macon City for the time being. At Macon City, the more strategic point, and the greater center of activity, there was constant movement of troops southward. And though the place was militarily held by the Federals, the Confederates were there too, and in very humble unmilitary plight, but having some work of their own to do. The movement of troops southward at this time was to reinforce General Halleck, who was in pursuit of General Price, retreating into Arkansas; and likewise to reinforce General Grant, who was massing men at Paducah and Columbus to march into Tennessee. North Missouri Railroad was the great artery for conveying troops from Iowa and Kansas to these southern battlefields.

In the midst of these events, and as a happy omen of cessation of warfare, multitudes of North Missourians, who had followed Price at Boonville, Wilson's Creek and Lexington, came flocking home; tired (as they said) of the war, and resolved henceforward to live and die in peace with all men. As a further proof of their peaceful and loyal intentions, they were very fond of staying near and around the Federal Camps, and of conversing with the Union Soldiers stationed at Macon City, Mexico and Sturgeon. They were never tired of dissuading all they met, from going to join Price, or of engaging in so wicked a war, as they called it. They preferred, they said, to stay near the Union camps, lest going home and scattering here and there unprotected, they would be liable to be murdered by roving bands of confederates for having deserted the confederate cause. All of a sudden their real purpose flashed out to heaven, in the light of all that was combustible of one hundred miles of the North Missouri Railroad, stretching out from Macon City towards St. Louis—ablaze at the same moment and as if ignited by one hand. Telegraph poles were cut down as if by the single stroke of an ax; and the wire, broken and in coils, was hauled away several miles, into the woods and fields. Bridges, culverts, trestles, tanks, station houses, were all set on fire. Yokes of oxen were harnessed to the ties, which were hauled out of place, then piled together to burn; and on the blazing heaps, the railroad iron, molten red in the center, fell down at the ends in crooks and twists, thereby rendering it unfit for use, until taken to some rolling mill or foundry to be straightened or recast. Not less than ten thousand men, acting in concert along that hundred miles, could have in the space of two or three hours produced so dire results. The plan was deep laid, the secret well kept, and the work thoroughly done. The confederate spies were soon back to their camp again, without loss of a man. The end of 1861 found me residing still at Macon City, to which place, as already stated, I had moved from Chillicothe after the fall of Lexington. My change of place of residence, in so far as I had hoped to be in greater safety, was a disappointment. The one hundred miles of burning railroad, between me and St. Louis, showed clearly that the smoke of battle had changed from front to rear. So "about face" I marched back again to Chillicothe.

CHAPTER XIV

STRAIGHTENING THE TWIGS.

THE financial straits, together with the civil and social disturbances caused by the war, brought the educational interests of the country into a very disorganized condition. In the rural districts and country towns the schools without funds or teachers, were generally suspended. In consequence, the children, instead of acquiring the learning and disciplined habits necessary for them, went about idle and un-instructed, associating with dangerous companions, and engaging in the exciting war talk everywhere prevalent at the time. The girls swayed by the party bias of their parents and relatives, contended with their companions, and often in angry words, as their preferences or family ties allied them to one or the other of the warring sections. The boys, breaking away from all restraint, formed opposing camps, and under their chosen leaders, assaulted each other with as varying results of victory or defeat, as the armies at Richmond and Shiloh. In this state of things the parents, Catholic and non-Catholic alike, besought me to take the children under my care, and to rescue them from the disorderly habits in which they were growing up. I could not but promise to do whatever I could for the dear children and their fond parents. Accordingly, I appointed a day for opening school in the Seminary building, which belonged to the town people, and which, in its battered neglected state, was fast going into ruin. On opening day it was a pleasing sight to see all the gay happy children flocking from all directions toward the school, their books, slates and papers in satchels over their shoulders, or carried under their arms. I was glad to see all the dear children, and in the fullness of my heart's joy, as I met them, they could see that they were received, bow for bow and smile for smile. How to take care of so many, and attend to my missions, was a puzzle to me. But I could not abandon the children, seeing how they panted for the pleasures of school. So I formed them into classes, according to their acquirements and capabilities, as I could judge them. The classes I placed under the more advanced pupils as teachers, and of these I made myself teacher in their advanced studies, with the understanding clearly impressed upon the minds of all, that I would personally supervise each and every class, and would carefully ascertain and make note of the standing and progress of each and every pupil in the several classes. Giving Saturdays and Sundays to the missions, I could devote five days of the week to the school. The work took onset, on and on it went. Catechism, Bible History, Greek, Latin, French, Rhetoric, Geometry, Algebra, Grammar,

Elocution, Philosophy, Reading, Writing, Arithmetic, Lessons in Music, went on unceasingly, as whirring machinery in a great factory or cotton mill. Ha, Ha, I had got the hopeful twigs where I could bend them to some purpose. And with the strain on them, ever urging them on, there was no longer any time for fugues or refrains or parrying thrusts about Yankeedom or Dixie. It was a matter next to life worth contending for, to stand well in class, and to keep an eye on the rewards that were surely to be given only to those who merited them well.

MY GENTLE LAMBS.

For two years and until the Public School system could be reorganized, my school went on, held on firmly and steadily; the excellent behavior and marked progress of the children a delight to me, and an ever increasing incentive to devote myself more and more to their interests and happy aspirations. I flatter myself that school was not in Chillicothe before or since, more successfully carried on, or more blessed with good order and mutual love of teachers and pupils. And I have reason to believe, too, that this mutual love still lingers on, abiding and undiminished; for never does any of these dear pupils meet me without manifesting the kindest and most reverential feelings for their old teacher. From those dear days of long ago, I treasure fondly in my mind, the most tender recollections of the good children, who never merited a word of reproach from my lips, or the gentlest slap from my hand. Now in my declining years it is one of my greatest pleasures to call to mind each well remembered name, with the personal appearance and traits of character to each belonging, of boy or girl. Often, too, I follow them in their diverging pathways of life, so far as it is given to me to know their history. But alas! many of them have gone from us forever, to a better world as I trust, to hear their names called as I fondly hope from the Book of Life.

THE ROLL CALL.

Pocahontas Bell, resides in Kansas City; married Z. A. Cooper, president Citizen's National Bank, Kansas City.

Rebecca Bell, resides in Kansas City; married George Lapsley, merchant, Kansas City.

Victor Bell, resides in Kansas City, capitalist; married Miss Lockridge.

Nannie Preston, resides in Trenton, Kentucky; conducts a Young Ladies Academy; married Professor Z. Vineyard.

Jennie Preston, died many years ago, at Grassy Valley, Livingston County, Missouri.

Mary Murray, Mother Mary William, Superior of Sisters of Mercy, Louisville, Kentucky; superintends a Young Ladies Academy and five parish schools in Louisville.

John H. Sullivan, superintendent Memphis & Birmingham Railroad; resides at Memphis.

Mary Catherine Dunne, Mother Mary Agnes; Superior Sisters of Mercy, 510 East 6th Street, Kansas City, Missouri.

S. S. Saunder, Cowen Lumber Co., Kansas City, Missouri.

C. I. Waples, Kevil & Waples, Furniture and Upholstery Merchants, Kansas City, Missouri.

Charles II. Shirley, son of Major Shirley, Chillicothe; volunteered for the Union Army at the close of school in the summer of 1864; killed in battle at Franklin Tennessee, Nov. 30, 1864.

Nicholas Hayes, died in Texas many years ago.

Lucinda Manning, resides at Chillicothe, Mo.

Cecilia Manning, resides in Kansas City; married Henry McLaine.

William Turner, lawyer; married; resides at Chillicothe, Missouri.

Lambert Manning, resides at Chillicothe, Mo.

Margaret Carlan, married, resided at St. Louis; in company with her husband set out on a tour of Europe; fell sick and died at Liverpool.

Rose Carlan, married, resides at St. Louis.

William Samuel, resides at Chillicothe, Mo.

Robert Samuel, lawyer, married, resides at Chillicothe, Missouri.

Alice Samuel, married, resides at Chillicothe, Mo.

Francis Tanner, married, resides at Chillicothe, Mo.

James Tanner, lives on a farm near Chillicothe.

Mary Leone Eales, married, lives at Sedalia, Mo.

John Eales, lives at Sedalia, Missouri.

John Moore, died many years ago at Brookfield, Missouri.

Margaret Moore, married, lives in Kansas.

Augustine Tooey, telegraph operator at Omaha.

Thomas Tooey, married, lives at Brookfield, Mo.

Lizzie Butcher, died many years ago at St. Joseph, Missouri.

Ellen Galvin, Sister of Humility of Mary, Ottumwa, Iowa.

Mary King, lives in St. Louis.

Of the following dear children, where they are, how they have fared in life, whether they be living or dead, I have no account whatever. Many there are, too, my failing memory cannot recall.

Mollie Walker,	James Walker,
Susan Walker,	Wilbur F. Gibson,
Philip Walker,	Jennie B. Gibson,
John Walker,	Sarah Cobb,
Jennie Swayne,	John McNicholas,
Betty Swayne,	John Dunham,
Buchanan Manning,	Emeline Dunham,
Thomas Swayne,	Belle Webb,
John Walsh,	Lucinda Webb,
Martin Walsh,	Fannie Harl,
Sarah Wittenberg,	Laura Shook,
Fanny Jamison,	Belle Grimes,
Alexander Jamison,	Margaret Francis,
William Jamison,	John Doss,

Charles Powell,	Margaret Cunningham,
Joseph King,	James Cunningham,
Catherine Angel,	Ellen Cunningham,
Julia Schoonover,	South West,
Charles H. Lehman,	May West,
Franklin Richards,	Lizzie West,
Mollie King,	Sarah Ellswick,
Cicero Sherman,	Martha F. Bevel,
Francis Sherman,	George F. Bevel,
Gilpin Brant,	Mary Galvin,
Margaret McGrogan,	Michael Galvin,

Thomas B. Hartgrove.

CHAPTER XV

BUSHWHACKERS AND GUERILLAS.

THE dangers encountered in travelling through Missouri, increased rather than lessened with the continuing years of the war. According as the contending armies moved southward, the territory they vacated became a prey to roving bands of murderers and robbers, privateers in the Confederate cause, who made raids for revenge and plunder. In North Missouri, the counties of Linn, Chariton, Boone and Randolph, suffered most from these wicked men. But the cruelest of their deeds was the massacre at Centralia in September, 1864, of which I barely escaped being a victim.

A PERILOUS NIGHT.

Saturday, September 24, 1864, I set out from Chillicothe by train to Macon City, where I was to change cars for Mexico, in Andrain County, the point of my destination; intending to celebrate Mass there next day, Sunday, the third Sunday of the month, which I usually gave to Mexico. At Macon City where it was well known I would be on the train that day, as I was changing cars, I was met by a messenger sent to intercept me for a sick call some miles distant in the country. I could not refuse attending the sick call, though attending it would necessarily cause me to lose the train then under full steam to set out for Mexico—and the only train going there before Monday. The great disappointment to the Catholics gathering from far and near at Mexico on the third Sunday of the month, which was the Sunday set apart for them, disconcerted me in my willing efforts for their sake, for they were pious good christians. Yet to abandon them was a duty in order not to deprive the dying Christian of the last helps of religion. The sick call attended, I returned to Macon City about sunset, with the grim determination on my features to make a night journey by hand car to Mexico, sixty miles distant. I knew that I could depend on the railroad section men to carry me, by successive relays from place to place, over the distance. The Macon City section men, informed of my purpose, although tired after the day's work, hastily partook of supper, and well oiling the heavy machinery of their hand car, put it on the track and put me on it with them, and then we were away, speeding southward on our journey. In an hour we had passed over their section of the road, ten miles to Jacksonville. The Jacksonville men soon had their handcar on the track, and we rode on it, in an hour, ten miles to Allen, which place is now called Moberly. The Allen men made their run of ten miles in an hour to Renick. The Renick men, asleep when we called on them, were soon up and out on the track, and away on the course. Instantly, in the flash of our headlight lantern, we saw armed men ahead of us, with levelled revolvers calling us to a halt. We halted. A number of them mounted our handcar, and with a harsh command to us from their captain to go on, on we went. They stayed on our handcar for several miles, not saying a word the while. Again the captain cried, halt. We halted. They alighted, and ordered us to go on. We went on, glad to be free, not knowing whether they were friends or foes who had pressed us into their service. As they wore no uniforms we conjectured they were guerillas, probably belonging to the band that had robbed Huntsville in that neighborhood the day previous, and now very likely reconnoitering the federal force encamped at Sturgeon, some miles before us. We went on to the Sturgeon outposts, where we were halted by the pickets, and by them taken to camp headquarters, where, having given satisfactory account of ourselves, we got a written order to pass through the federal lines and beyond the camp. It was now midnight, and there yet remained twenty-two miles journey before us. The next relay of men took me eight miles, to Centralia. The Centralia men, aroused from their slumbers, soon had their handcar on the track, and with them I proceeded over the intervening distance, twelve miles, to Mexico; where, arrived at half past two o'clock Sunday morning, I was once again, as at Sturgeon, halted by the federal pickets, and by them taken to camp headquarters, where, having satisfactorily accounted for myself, I was again furnished with a military pass to go through the lines. I now had on my person three federal military passes, the first one having been given me a considerable time previous by Provost Marshal General McKinstry, of St. Louis, as a necessary condition to pass beyond the lines of that city.

SUNDAY'S BLESSED DAWN.

The blessed twilight of Sunday morning, September 25, streamed in upon me as I knelt before the altar in the parlor of a private residence in Mexico, where as yet we had no church. Having recited the Matins, Lauds, and Little Hours of the Divine Office, I was prepared to begin the duties of hearing confessions, preparatory to the celebration of Holy Mass. Gradually the people began to arrive, and soon not only the chapel parlor but likewise the halls and adjoining rooms were entirely filled. All seemed anxious to receive the holy sacraments, for which they had been; during the previous month devoutly preparing themselves; and all the more so as in those dangerous times, life was very uncertain. Their wishes were gratified. At Mass nearly all who were present partook of the Holy Communion. After thanksgiving, at which no doubt many fervent prayers were offered up to God for heavenly favors, according to each one's pressing needs, and especially for the restoration of peace, they departed quietly for their homes, some of them having to go a long distance into the country. When all had gone, I, too, resumed my missionary journey, going that evening fourteen miles farther south, to Martinsburg, the remotest station from Chillicothe of the district I attended. Next morning I said Mass, likewise at a private house, at Martinsburg, for the little congregation then beginning to gather there. After Mass, having partaken of some refreshment, I prepared myself to travel on the daily north bound train from St. Louis, that was to take me before sunset, one hundred and thirty-four miles, to my distant home at Chillicothe.

OH, THE HORRID CRIME.

The train from St. Louis arrived in due time at Martinsburg Station, and having taken a seat in one of the coaches, I was soon reversing the journey I had made two nights previous on the handcars. Nothing unusual transpired on the way until we had reached Centralia, where, as the train was passing out from the Station, a troop of horsemen, moving rapidly across the prairie north of us, came in sight, halted, and quickly formed a line facing the train. Knowing well from their appearance, and as they wore no uniform, that they were guerillas, we feared a volley from their guns every moment. In anticipation of this, some federal soldiers who were aboard the train, brought their muskets to a ready to return the volley. But there was no firing, however; the

train having passed quickly out of range. These
armed horsemen were, no doubt, outposts from Bill
Anderson's guerillas, four hundred strong, then encamped in the woods and ravines in sight of Centralia, and waiting for an opportunity to attack some
passing train. The ill-fated train that the attack fell
on was the first following the one I was on. It came
along the next day at noon. As it approached the
Centralia Station, the guerillas with savage yells
rushed out from their hiding places, and throwing
obstructions on the track, commenced firing on the
train which had to stop. Then the robbing began.
Money, gold watches, jewelry, were dragged off the
persons and pulled from the pockets of the passengers, men and women, indiscriminately. The express
safe was broken open and rifled. Packages and
boxes of express goods, and trunks were broken open
and emptied of their valuables. A number of federal
soldiers on the train were ordered out, put into line,
and shot dead on the spot. A major of the federal
army commanding one hundred and fifty mounted
men, sallied out from a neighboring military post to
give battle to the guerillas. These being vastly in
majority and likewise better armed and equipped, fell
upon the federals and slew them almost to a man.
The railroad train, depot, and cars, were fired and
burned. Never was there a more heart-rending scene
of carnage and devastation; and for the like of it, for
cold-blooded cruel atrocity, we look in vain in the

annals of military history, even of savage nations. Had I waited or been delayed at Martinsburg or Mexico for that train, and had the federal military passes that I carried, been found on me, which certainly would have happened, as the pockets and pocket-books of all passengers were searched, there is no doubt whatever that I would have shared the fate of the poor fellows who fell on that occasion. Ever and always has the hand of God seemed raised over me, to protect me from otherwise unavoidable disaster and danger. To God's infinite mercy I owe my life saved hundreds of times.

CHAPTER XVI.

BOGUS—AMERICANS.

IN the last stages of the war the perpetration of a great wrong was attempted by the radical party then in power in Missouri, which resulted in a clear demonstration of the utter incapacity and untrustworthiness of that party to govern this great nation according to their principles. In November, 1864, the proposition to hold a State Convention for the purpose of amending the State Constitution was voted by a large majority. The Convention met in January, 1865. The business before it was the emancipation of slaves and the qualifications for voters, which were clearly within purview of Civil Government. But the Convention did not confine itself to the range of its powers and duties, or to the purposes it was called for. Forgetting the cardinal principle of American jurisprudence and government—not to interfere with the exercise of religion, the Convention got itself into the predicament of the cobbler going beyond his last. The Convention sat from January 6th to April 10th, and fittingly selected Fool's Day for the fool's job. Accordingly, on April 1st, Fool's Day the world over, the wiseacres formulated penalties of fine and imprisonment against bishop, priest, minister, elder, or clergyman of any religious persuasion, sect or denomination, who would teach, or preach, or solemnize marriage, unless on compliance with conditions prescribed by civil authority. The law went into force July 4, 1865. But to accommodate the clergy, they were given sixty days grace, that is to say, until September 3 inclusive, in which to make, subscribe and file the oath that was to ordain them lawful gospellers.

TESTING OUR METTLE.

On Sunday, September 4th, the first day after the sixty day's grace had elapsed, I was in Chillicothe; and, not having taken, subscribed, or filed the preacher's oath, I preached three times that day; at first Mass, at high Mass, and at Vespers, not saying a word however regarding the oath. Not content with my modicum of zeal, I requested the Reverend William Kelly, of Columbus, Nebraska, then staying with me on a visit, to preach at Benediction, at half past seven in the evening. "Oh, with great pleasure," he replied; "you do me great honor, inviting me with you to the penitentiary." So we had four sermons that day, when otherwise we would have had but one. My perversity went on, though I never doubted that my day of reckoning would come. It came, but not without dishonorable methods. The November Term of the Circuit Court was drawing near, and as usual a Grand Jury was sworn in, as follows: George W. McMillen, Jacob R. Houch, Joseph S.

Baxter, David Stone, Joseph W. West, Charles Hart, William Thomas, John Green, Howard S. Harbaugh, William S. Davis, D. C. Bucklin, Robert W. Cullough, Josiah B. Cooper, and James R. Sullivan: Foreman, George W. McMillen. These Grand Jurors sat from Nov. 20th to Dec. 13th. But, as they failed, and positively refused, to see crimes and misdemeanors in the light of the new radical law, they shared the fate of the "Long Parliament," were driven out with objurgations, by a Cromwell, at their back. Poor Jury System! What art thou, after all thy vaunted glory, when the wave of a tyrant's hand can unmake thee! Praesto! the tyrant's hand beckons, and in comes the "Praise God Barebones" Jury, as follows: Martin J. Jenkins, Daniel J. Mecum, Louis Brown, Horatio G. Hallowell, John M. Alexander, Jared McIrvin, William H. Messman, Percil Brinkerhoff, Pleasant Odil, Benjamin Hargrave, Thomas J. Reed, Daniel Wallbrunn, John Shook, Thornton Russell, Thomas Mitchell, James Veatch, Alexander Noble: Foreman; John M. Alexander. The "Bare Bones" Jury had hardly taken their seats before they found against Rev. John Hogan, as follows.

INDICTMENT.

The State of Missouri, 17th Judicial Circuit, in the Circuit Court of Livingston County, November Term, A. D., 1865, begun and held on the 20th day of November, A. D., 1865. Livingston County, to wit:

The Grand Jurors for the State of Missouri, in and for the body of the County of Levingston aforesaid, being duly empanelled and sworn, upon their oath present, that John Hogan on the third day of December, A. D., 1865, at said county, was a priest of a religious persuasion and sect called the Roman Catholic Church, and at the County aforesaid, and on the day and year last aforesaid, the said John Hogan did unlawfully and with force and arms, exercise the functions of Priest by preaching to divers persons whose names are to the Jury unknown, and that at the time the said John Hogan so exercised the functions of priest as aforesaid, more than sixty days had elapsed from the time of the taking effect of the present constitution of the State of Missouri, and the said John Hogan had not at the time he exercised and performed the functions aforesaid, taken, subscribed and filed the oath of loyalty prescribed by and contained in the 6th Section of the 2nd article of the constitution of the said State, contrary to the form of the statute in such case made and provided, and against the peace and dignity of the State.

John Dixon, County Attorney and Circuit Attorney Pro Tem. Upon the indictment are the following endorsements, to wit:

The State of Missouri versus John Hogan. Indictment for exercising functions of priest without having taken, subscribed and filed the oath of loyalty.

John M. Alexander,
Foreman of the Grand Jury.

Names of Witnesses:
Michael O'Brien,   Peter Markey.
Filed Dec. 14, 1865.   R. F. Dunn, Clerk.

CATCH HIM FIRST.

There is an old saying, that to cook a hare you must catch him first. I was the hare. The Missouri Radicals no doubt intended to cook me. And naturally enough I made up my mind, that the harriers at my heels, should take some twists and turns and doubles with me, before I would be finally run down. In a word, there was to be some fun at the hunt. I am unwilling to say, or rather have not the humility to deny, that this was the wiser or more proper course to follow. And had anyone preached to me, that I should have turned the unsmitten cheek to share the fate of the smitten one, I fear I would have pertly replied, that I had been already slapped on both cheeks. Anyhow I was not in want of good precept or good example. An exemplary lady of my congregation having like myself a liberal Hibernian education, seeing her husband who had taken his glass too freely, going to jail in the hands of the police, to whom he was giving a good kicking for their impudence. cried out to him: "Michael; Michael; go daycint; go daycint." As I had a good deal of Michael's temper in me I did not think it manly to "go daycint" to jail in the hands of the radicals.

So it happened that I had made up my mind to do some kicking.

"A MAN'S ENEMIES HIS OWN HOUSEHOLD."

However when the time for kicking came, I found myself in the predicament of the mother, whose own children were in mischief, and whose heart would let her raise but a straw on high over their heads to beat them with. I had a very good choir in my beautiful little church at Chillicothe. Two estimable young ladies, fond sisters they were, graduates of a convent, were the Prima Donnas. Mozart, Hayden, Beethoven, and Lambilotte's music was a familiar study to these gifted songstresses and accomplished performers. The elder one particularly excelled in music and singing, and took great interest in advancing the efficiency of the choir. She got married to the sheriff of the county, who, as might be expected, was a frequent attendant at, although not a member of, the church where his wife sang. The deputy sheriff, too, a modest much respected young gentleman, familiarly known by the pleasing name of "Drury," joined the choir, and was much devoted to singing in the church, of which however he was not a member. If it was against the law for me to preach without having taken the Test Oath, I can certainly aver that the sheriff and his lady and the deputy sheriff too, did help me very materially in my wickedness, for they sang more than the Amen's to my disloyal worship. And yet it was that same sweet "Drury" that came to arrest me for carrying on divine worship "by force and arms, and against the peace and dignity of the State," of which crime he was himself as guilty as I was. But he honestly tried for my sake, to make my arrest a sugar-coated affair.

DRURY DEAR, HOW ARE YOU?

On the last day but one of the year 1865, which was Saturday, my modest young chorister riding an elegant horse, drew up at the gate before my cottage. Dismounting, he passed gracefully on foot through the grassy lawn, amid cedars and arbor vitae, that led up to the door. I saw him as he advanced. His dress and manner were faultless, but his bland smile had left him, and his face was as solemn and woebegone as if he had come to invite me to his father's funeral. Hastening to meet him, I said: "Drury dear, how are you; and why are you so grave and serious to-day?"

"Have you not heard the bad news," said he.

"No," said I, "what is it?"

"You have been indicted," said he; "the Grand Jury have found against you, for having preached without having taken the test oath. Garry and I are afraid the constable will take you to jail, as he may do at any moment; and to prevent this disgrace we have thought it better to call upon you without delay, and to have you sign a bond for your appearance. But you need not go to court until Term time, which will be the third Monday in May next."

"Thank you, Drury," said I; "the news is not the worst possible. Garry and you take much of the harm out of it. And, so you tell me, my friend Garry Harker, the sheriff, has sent you here with all possible speed, so as to be first to do me a favor?"

"Yes," said he.

"And have you the bond?" said I.

"Yes," said he, "here it is."

"Thanks be to Garry," said I; "it is very kind of him to be so thoughtful of me. Drury, please wait here a minute until I return from the next room."

"At your pleasure," said Drury, bowing politely.

"LIST, LIST, O LIST!"
HAMLET.

Having softly closed the door between myself and Drury, I quickly dressed in full canonicals—Soutane, surplice, stole, birette; then taking a large crucifix in my right hand, and in my left a large Folio Bible, which I swung over my shoulder, I opened the door and advanced towards Drury, saying to him in a low but rather commanding voice: "Now, sir, I am ready for you; come along." Instantly there was a scene. Drury rose to his feet, and with horrified face and outstretched hands, seemed to fall into the role of Hamlet before the Ghost, though his lips spoke not a syllable.

"Angels and ministers of grace defend us. Be thou spirit or goblin? Thou comest in such a questionable shape. I WILL speak to thee. O, answer me. What may this mean? Say, why is this?"

"Drury," said I, " I am a priest; I plead guilty; I confess that I preached the gospel without authority from the State to do so; and if I will have to go to jail for it, you will have to take me there. That's what's the matter."

"But," said Drury, "if you please, go to the Court House without me. You will please take that street, and I will take this, and when we meet at the Court House, we will fix up this bond there."

"Drury," said I, "you were never ashamed of me before, now you will not walk with me. What have I done to you that you are so displeased with me? If you go without me, you know you will have to come after me again."

But, Reverend Father," said Drury, "please ride my horse and I will walk."

"Oh, not so, dear Drury; this canonical dress is not becomingly worn on horseback. Rather do you ride and I will walk with you." So we paired, side by side. He on horseback, I, "in the name of the Lord." O, the crowds, the crowds, that gathered up, and followed us from all sides. I feared, as there was anger visible, and excitement all around, that there would be trouble. But who could think of interfering when it was seen that Drury and I were friendly, and when it was very well known that we were dear friends. Yet, at one time on the march along the street, with hundreds of people at our heels, there was danger, as an old negro lady moaned out: "Oh Lor' have mercy, there is Father Hogan going to jail, and Drury McMillen has him prisoner." But Drury was fond of me, and I was fond of Drury. So, I went with him to the Court House, and signed the bond. We bade each other good bye. He went to his home. I, too, went home to change my canonical dress for less ghostly attire. Then I went to the depot to take train for Cameron, where I was to say Mass the following day—the fifth Sunday of the month, the last day of the year 1865.

CHAPTER XVII

THE RING OF THE TRUE METAL.

THE dramatic scene between Drury and myself had the happy effect of allaying much of the excitement and wounding shame the arrest had caused. But the Catholic people were not to be soothed or palavered by any by-play in the matter. To say that the deepest anger and indignation had swayed them, would not half portray the intensity of their feelings. To the Catholics of Brookfield and Linn County belong the honor and high distinction of being the first, and so far as I know the only people in the State of Missouri, to call a public meeting, to denounce, oppose and resist, the infamous, anti-christian measures of the Missouri Radical Constitution, and to brand it with the condemnation of public scorn. And if there be any who doubt that those who first unfurled the flag of religious liberty in America, do not mean to keep that flag with its proud folds fluttering defiantly in the breeze, let them read what the people of that Faith have put on record at Brookfield. It has always been a cause of great regret to me that I had no share in the honor of that meeting, which I was unable to attend, having been called elsewhere on important

missionary duty.   But the proceedings show that my
presence was not needed, and that the courage, in-
spiration and resolution of the men who composed
it, could not have been heightened by mortal man,
no matter how exalted his station.   A deputation
from the Brookfield meeting waited on me at Chillicothe to lay the proceedings before me, which are
as follows.

THE BROOKFIELD MEETING.

"Reverend and Dear Sir: At a meeting held by the
Catholics of Linn County, at Brookfield, on the 6th
day of February, 1866, we were deputed to apprise
you of the following resolutions, then and there
adopted:

Whereas our Pastor, Rev. John Hogan, has been
indicted by a Grand Jury of Livingston County, and
held for trial as a criminal for preaching the Gospel
of Jesus Christ:

And whereas we feel it to be our duty to express
our opinion publicly of the act; therefore be it
resolved:

1st; That we consider the introduction of a Test
Oath into the Constitution of this State as an in-
fringement of civil and religious liberty, as taught
and expounded by the revered founders of this
Republic.

2nd; That the leading object in incorporating this
oath in the Constitution, with the provision affecting
the tenure of church property, and that authorizing

the levy of taxes on churches, charitable institutions and the graves of the dead, so unbecoming a Christ ian and civilized people, is believed by us to be aimed especially at our religion, which has labored to rear in this state, for the common good, and to the con- fusion of the infidel only, so many noble institutions of Faith, Education, Benevolence and Charity.

3rd; That regarding, as we do, Religion to be the only means of promoting our eternal happiness, and of remedying the great moral evils that afflict society, we will not support any party whose object is to interfere with or crush religion.

4th; That we know and testify, in common with all our fellow citizens, of every religious denomina- tion and political opinion, that there was not, and could not have been, a more strictly loyal man to his government in the time of its sore trial, than he who is now held in the grip of power, and prejudged to punishment, to the great detriment of law, which ought to be a terror, not to the good, but to evil- doers.

5th; That we regard the arrest of the Reverend John Hogan as an act of unmitigated tyranny, alike revolting to our feelings and provoking to our pas- sions; and that we do here now publicly rebuke that act, in itself, and in its agents and abettors, as a most shameful and atrocious outrage.

6th; That we do and shall sustain our pastor in his efforts to maintain inviolate the sacred principles of religious liberty as a God-given right; and that we regard him as the successor of those fearless men, who, in the history of the past, stood face to face with the hangman and the headsman, choosing the agony of the axe, the halter and the gibbet, rather than submit to any governmental test, to qualify them to preach Christ's sacred Gospel, or subscribe to the supremacy of the civil power over Christ's spiritual Kingdom.

7th; That we hereby appoint Patrick Tooey, John McCormick, John Curtin, and William O'Neil, a committee to inform the said Reverend John Hogan, our pastor, of the sense and action of this meeting, and to present to him a testimonial from us, indicative of our heart-felt sympathy with him in his sufferings, and our high appreciation of his firm and unflinching conduct.

8th; That a copy of these proceedings be furnished for publication to the newspapers of Linn and Livingston counties; and likewise to the St. Louis Republican, St. Louis Dispatch, St. Louis Guardian, and Boston Pilot.

Brookfield, Missouri, February 6th, 1866.

James Tooey,

Chairman.

Michael White,

Secretary.

You will now perceive, Reverend and Dear Sir, that the reading of these resolutions does but partly accomplish the task entrusted to us. There yet remains for us the more pleasing duty, of putting into your hands this purse, which you will find not meager or destitute of pecuniary resources to aid you. Furthermore, we beg of you to accept it as a present from ourselves and those whom we represent. We have the honor to be, Rev. and Dear Sir, your obedient servants.

<table>
<tr><td>John McCormick,</td><td>Patrick Tooey,</td></tr>
<tr><td>Thomas Bresnahan,</td><td>John Curtin,</td></tr>
</table>

William O'Neil,

Committee.

REPLY TO THE BROOKFIELD DELEGATION.

Gentlemen: I thank you for your encouraging words and generous present. Your kindness imposes on me the obligation of devoting myself anew to the defence of your principles. You term Religious Liberty a God-given right. So it is. Let me add. You need not thank anyone but God for it. God is the source of Right and Power. He has said to those sent by Him to teach His religion: "All power is given to me in heaven and in earth. Going therefore teach ye all nations. And behold I am with you all days, even to the consummation of the world." In virtue of this power, He sends us to teach, and promises to be with us. His authority is ours. Were it man's authority, man would not now oppose, nor from the beginning have opposed, its exercise. The Civil Authority has been, ever from the days of Herod, the enemy of Christ. Christ therefore could not have entrusted to it, the care of His heavenly teaching. He appointed others besides civil rulers for this purpose. By His appointees He has stood unto this present day; and by them, as sure as His word faileth not, He will stand until the end of the world. It is very foolish then in the Civil Government, to assume an authority that does not belong to it, and to declare in contravention of God's ordination, who shall or shall not preach or teach the Gospel of Christ. This rash assumption of authority by the Civil Government, in a matter that does not belong to it, and over which it has no control, is as weak, silly, and tyrannical as the act of Xerxes, flogging with chains the tossing waves of the sea to make them do his will. One would think that the Civil Power would now at least in this more enlightened age of the world, cease its impotent rage against the Church, knowing as it does after its many defeats, vain struggles and humiliations, that the Church will obey only its maker, and that chains and prisons have no terror for it. And if we should prove recreant to our duty in this respect, we would accomplish nothing for the Civil Power thereby. The liberty of perdition would be of no avail to us or to it. Against us and against it, Christ would still maintain His Church. He would raise up others in our place, who would obey His voice and do His will. In obeying the Church and the state in their respective spheres, we are most obedient to law.

We obey God first, our country next, and ourselves last. It is the inversion of these principles that we fear, and that would work the greatest detriment to the State and civil society as well as the Church.

The question now pending is not one merely of loyalty or disloyalty, past, present or prospective. The issue is, whether the Church shall be free or not, to exercise her natural and inherent right, of calling into or rejecting from her ministry whom she pleases; whether yielding to the dictation of the civil power, she shall admit those only who, according to its judgment, are fit for the office; or, admitting these to be fit, whether she shall not be free to call in those also who, though at first not fit, afterwards become so through pardon and repentance.

The question is whether the Church is not as much at liberty, and as fully competent now-a-days, as at the beginning, to call in as well the saints as those who were sinners, as well the Baptist and Evangelist as St. Peter and St. Paul, the persecutor and denier of the Redeemer as well as his presanctified messenger and beloved desciple. With all these questions the State has nothing to do. Their decision is the high and unapproachable prerogative of the Church, under the guidance of her Redeemer, who alone is the searcher of hearts, and whose power it is to call in or reject whom He pleases.

And now before we part, let me bid you be neither despondent nor disheartened. God is with you; who then can be against you. The history of the past is the index to the future. What, though we be cast into prison? What, though pains and penalties await us? What, though cells and dungeons be multiplied to debar us from our liberty? Still, the victory of evil will not be complete. Liberty and truth, ever superior to force, will defy the torturer to subjugate them. The momentary triumph of the wicked and the cruel, will be branded with perpetual shame. And out from those dark dungeons and dreary cells, will shine forth a cheering light, to bid all good men hope, and to show by the contrast who are the truer friends of religion and country—they who uphold liberty by the sacrifice of themselves, or they who sacrifice liberty to the unauthorized control of a usurping power. Be firm, yet patient, in the defence of right. This is the christian's struggle for the christian's crown. Let no violence characterize your actions as evil. Bless and pray for those who persecute you, for they are your rulers still. Respect and obey them, consistently with the reverence and obedience you owe to God. To-day, as of old, the religion you profess is ever the same. It bids you, if needs be, to die for Christ, but not conspire against Caesar.

Thanking you, Gentlemen, from the fullness of my grateful heart for your kindness and devotion, I pray God to bless you, and strengthen you with the armor of faith; yea with that faith that giveth victory and overcometh the world, that by it you may prevail against your enemies. May God bless you, the Father, and the Son, and the Holy Ghost. Amen.

ON THE ALTAR OF HIS COUNTRY.

About a dozen years previous to this (test oath) time, when assistant at St. John's Church, in St. Louis, having obtained permission to go on a short vacation for my health into the country, I accepted the kind invitation of a hospitable brother clergyman, to ride with him in his carriage to his home in Millwood, in Lincoln County. Delighted with the beautiful scenery of North Missouri, which I then beheld for the first time, I continued my happy wanderings through woodland and prairie, day after day, and often in the starry twilight hours, until at length I found myself in Ralls County, close by the far famed stream, sacred to the Manes of discomfited politicians; on the shores of which stood, as I was told, the classic town of Cincinnati. Having found not the town but the place where the geographies said it was, or ought to be, I next turned my attention to looking for the venerable personage himself, after whom the town was named. Ascending a hill, I surveyed the outlying transflumenal shore; and there, sure enough, Cincinnatus, bright as fancy could paint him, stood before me, cultivating with spade and hoe, his little farm of four jugera, clad in humble tunic only, his official toga thrown carelessly across a hickory stump, and not expecting of course to be called forth by his fellow citizens to be the savior of his country.

Strange to say, this same historical personage came across my pathway once again, some years later, not in fancy, as at Salt River, in Ralls County, but in reality on the banks of Grand River, in Livingston County, in the State of Missouri; and as chance would have it, it was during the canvass for votes preceding an exciting election, at which, amongst other high offices, a judgeship was to be bestowed on the successful candidate for popular favor.

Our Cincinnatus was once a limb of the law, in which he would have people believe, he was mightily versed and successful, but the practice of which he had given up because, as he said, it had deprived him of the pleasure of mingling as freely as he would wish with the working classes, whose society he very much preferred. Now, however, to serve these good people, who were not, as he told them, as fully represented on the bench as they should be, he was willing to give up his happy retirement, and forego the healthful pleasures of hoeing corn, splitting rails and going around into blacksmith's and carpenter's shops with hatchets and spades to helve, and axes to grind. In a word, he was willing to don the toga and the ermine, if the favoring attention of his friends would but bestow the official honor upon him. Of course there was a hurrah, and "three cheers and a tiger," for the candidate who was so willing to sacrifice himself on the altar of his country. In other respects, too, he had a special fitness for the administration of justice, as that sacred duty was understood at the time. He excelled in grilling Papists for being, as he called them, followers of the man of Sin at Rome, and in pursuing copper-heads, suspected of sympathies with persons south of Mason and Dixon's line. He was the man for the times— the times when Radical bayonets held the polls for Radicals. Not a doubt of it. Brother Jonas was triumphantly elected. Forthwith a delegation went to fetch him from his little hut on the four acre patch. Whereupon, taking up once again his aristrocratic toga, from the hickory stump on which he had put it out to air, for as you know he never intended to put it on his shoulders again; then, with the fasces borne before him, he proceeded to the dread judgment seat, with power of life and death in his hands. His first act was to drive out the Copper Head Grand Jury, as he called them, and give their places to the "Praise God Bare Bones" Grand Jury; who, as already said, instantly indicted me for having preached the Gospel without State license. Seeing all this, and sorely smitten in conscience—wicked, unlawful gospeler that I was—I bowed my head meekly and smote my breast contritely, saying, unhappy man that I am, "my cake is baked!"

BEFORE THE JUDGMENT SEAT.

On Wednesday, May 23rd, 1866, at Regular May Term, I was arraigned in the Criminal Court at Chillicothe, to answer to the charge of having exercised the functions of Priest by preaching, without having first taken, subscribed and filed the oath prescribed by the Missouri Convention. Before pleading began I had been notified that witnesses were voluntarily present in Court, to make affidavit, that the Judge on the Bench by whom my case was to be tried, had made a speech at a public meeting in Chillicothe, in which he assailed Roman Catholics as opposed to the institutions and government of the country. This information was communicated at once to the counsel who had generously, without hope or promise of pay or price undertaken my defense; Honorable Mordecai Oliver of St. Joseph, late Sec'y of State of Missouri; and Honorable James McFerrin, of Gallatin, late Colonel Missouri United States Volunteers; both, eminent as statesmen and jurists. These gentlemen, as the first step in my defense, demurred to the indictment for several reasons, but chiefly for the reason, that the provisions of the constitution of Missouri, under which the proceedings were instituted, were repugnant to the constitution of the United States, and consequently void. The points of objection presented by the demurrer were ably and zealously argued by counsel; but the sapient judge on the bench, in harmony with his preconceived opinions and the prejudices of the times, overruled the demurrer with manifest satisfaction. In this conjuncture I was somewhat embarrassed, as a trial was

urged by the prosecuting attorney, and evidently desired by the judge of the court, and I had no defense
except the unconstitutionality of the proceedings, as
hereinbefore stated; and, besides, I had instructed my
counsel not to deny the facts, the acts charged, but
to defend upon high constitutional grounds. For I
was guilty of preaching and teaching as a priest of
the Catholic Church, as charged in the indictment,
without having first taken the oath as prescribed in
the State constitution of 1865; and I further instructed my counsel, that having received my authority to teach and preach from a higher and holier authority than state constitutions or state laws; I
should in the future continue to preach and teach in
accordance with the dictates of my own conscience,
in utter defiance of constitutions or laws, and trust
consequences to God Himself.

PERSECUTED IN ONE CITY, FLEE INTO ANOTHER.

Under these circumstances my counsel advised me
to take a change of venue, and a change was ordered.
Before, however, my case came on for trial in
another circuit, the Supreme Court of the United
States had decided the Father Cummings case, and
held as the counsel in my case held, the part of the
Missouri State Constitution hereinbefore referred to
was void, because repugnant to the constitution of
the United States. My case was sent to the Adair
Circuit Court, one hundred miles from Chillicothe.

On Sunday night, the 14th of October following,

after having spent the day in the discharge of my
pastoral duties to the congregation at Macon City, I
rode in a buggy thirty-six miles to Kirksville, the
county seat of Adair, there being no railroad between
these places at that time. In the morning, as I
sat to breakfast at the hotel in Kirksville, it was
whispered about by the guests, that I was the priest
from Livingston County, who was to be arraigned
that day for not having taken the Test Oath. Immediately a gentleman at table, of distinguished appearance, who, as I afterwards learned, was a lawyer
from St. Louis, made a rattling attack on me before
all present, to whom I was an entire stranger; charg-
ing me with giving seditious example by criminally
disobeying the laws of my country, and that in the
eyes of the world I was no clergyman deserving of
respect. I replied faintly, for I was disheartened
and tired, to the effect that the purpose of my journey of one hundred miles from Chillicothe to Kirksville, was to see first of all, whether in fact I was in
duty bound to obey a law, the lawfulness of which
being very obscure to my mind, I was obliged to call
in question.

Having partaken hastily of breakfast, which I
did not very much enjoy, as the eyes of all at table
were leveled at me, I arose, gave thanks, and hastened to the Court House. It was regular Term
Time. The October Term. Third Monday of October, October 15th, 1866.

IN THE ADAIR CIRCUIT COURT.

As I entered the Court House I found the Court already in session, and my case, the first on the docket, called for hearing. In answer to the call a dignified, venerable gentleman arose, and spoke as follows: "May it please the Court. I am not personally acquainted with the Reverend John Hogan, or Father Hogan as he is called. Nor am I retained by him as counsel. Nevertheless, I know him by reputation. And even though I did not know him by reputation, I know the cause for which he comes here, so far from his home. I am here to defend him and his cause." At this moment, perceiving that I had come into Court, he bowed to me, and was about to retire. At once I bowed most profoundly to him, and with evident delight and gratitude beaming on my features. Then, whispering to him aside, I requested him to motion the Court for a continuance of the case to the next term of Court, or until the decision in the Father Cummings case, which was the same as mine and then pending in the Supreme Court of the United States, would be rendered. The motion for a continuance was accordingly made, and unhesitatingly granted. Having given bond for my appearance at the next Term of Court, and having thanked the Honorable Gentleman who had volunteered to defend me, and who, as I learned, was Judge Ellison, of Canton, Missouri, I set out on the return journey to Macon, and from Macon by rail to my home at Chillicothe. Nothing now remained for me to do, but to await the decision in the Cummings case, for which the great legal lights of America, were soon to meet in combative argument at Washington.

CHAPTER XVIII

THE CUMMINGS CASE.

REV. John A. Cummings, pastor of the Catholic Church at Louisiana, Pike County, Missouri, exercised the functions of Priest at that place without having taken the Test Oath that became of obligation in Missouri after September 3, 1865. Forthwith he was arrested, indicted, and convicted in the Circuit Court of Pike County. He appealed to the Supreme Court of the State, where the judgment of the Circuit Court was affirmed. He then took his case to the United States Supreme Court on writ of error, where the case was argued in December, 1866. Hon. David Dudley Field, of New York, argued the case for Rev. John A. Cummings, Plaintiff. Hon. George P. Strong, of Missouri, argued for the State of Missouri, Defendant. Hon. J. B. Henderson, of Missouri, also argued for the State of Missouri, Defendant. Hon. Reverdy Johnson, of Maryland, argued for the plaintiff, Rev. John A. Cummings, in reply. The arguments are given in full in Cummings vs. the State of Missouri, United States Supreme Court reports 71, Wallace 4.

HONORABLE REVERDY JOHNSON.

The fame of Honorable Reverdy Johnson as a

pleader and jurist of more than national reputation, was greatly enhanced by the praise and favorable comment bestowed on him from all sides for his argument on this memorable occasion. And yet, there are men of eminent legal acumen who think, that in his argument he got beside himself, by the too wide admission; "The Constitution of the United States, to be sure, so far as the article which proclaims that there shall be no interference with religion is concerned, is not obligatory on the State of Missouri."

Reverdy Johnson went on to explain the worth and value of the Constitution of the United States: "It announces a great principle of American liberty, a principle deeply seated in the American mind, and now almost in the entire mind of the civilized world; that as between a man and his conscience, as relates to his obligation to God, it is not only tyrannical but un-christian to interfere. It is almost inconceivable, that in this civilized day, the doctrine contained in this (Missouri) constitution, should be considered as within the legitimate sphere of human power."

REPLY TO BROOKFIELD DELEGATION QUOTED.

Reverdy Johnson proceeded. "This question," it has been truly said by another Clergyman sought to be restrained by this Constitution, "is not one merely of loyalty or disloyalty, past, present or prospective. The issue is, whether the church shall be free or not, to exercise her natural and inherent right, of calling into or rejecting from her ministry whom she pleases; whether yielding to the dictation of civil power, she shall admit only those who, according to its judgment, are fit for the office; or, admitting these to be fit, whether she shall not be free to call in those also, who, though at first not fit, afterwards become so through pardon and forgiveness. The question is, whether the church is not as much at liberty, and as fully competent, now-a-days as at the beginning, to call in as well the saints as those who were sinners, as well the Baptist and Evangelist as St. Peter and St. Paul, the denier and persecutor of the Redeemer, as well as his presanctified messenger and beloved disciple. With all these questions the State has nothing to do. Their decision is the high and unapproachable prerogative of the church, under the guidance of its Redeemer, who alone is the searcher of hearts, and whose power it is to call in or reject whom He pleases."

UNITED STATES SUPREME COURT DECISION.

Judgment was rendered by Justice S. J. Field, substantially as follows: Article I Section 9 of the Constitution of the United States, says: No bill of attainder or ex-post-facto law shall be passed. A bill of attainder is a legislative act, which inflicts punishment without a judicial trial. The Missouri law presumes the guilt of clergymen, and adjudges them deprived of their rights, unless the presumption be removed by an expurgatory oath. The judgment of the Supreme Court of Missouri must be reversed, and it is so ordered, and the case remanded, with directions to enter a judgment of the Circuit Court, and directing that Court to discharge the defendant from imprisonment, and suffer him to depart without delay.

Judges sustaining the decision: S. F. Field, Samuel Nelson, R. C. Grier, N. Clifford, N. H. Swayne.

Judges dissenting: S. P. Chase, J. W. Swayne, S. F. Miller, David Davis.

Accordingly, Rev. John A. Cummings, of Louisiana, Pike County, Missouri, was discharged and suffered to go free. And, at the Adair Circuit Court, Missouri, May Term 1867; it being the 27th May, 1867; the case against Rev. John Hogan, of Chillicothe, Missouri, was dismissed; and the said Rev. John Hogan was suffered to depart at will.

CHAPTER XIX.

"IN NOTHING BE YE TERRIFIED
Philippians, 1:28.

THE diablerie of the Missouri Test Oath, against which I fought to the end, had no terrorizing power to compare with that inspired by a very ferocious character, with whom I had to wage a hand to hand encounter a short time previous. Everyone who believes in revelation, believes that there is one whom revelation purposes to overthrow, and whose existence makes revelation necessary. This one that revelation is pursuing, is known "as a murderer from the beginning." (St. John 8:44. Timid people, and those who desire to be particularly polite, call him "The Bad Man;" but his true name, as he was called long ages ago, and as he should be now called, is Lucifer, Satan, the Devil. He rebelled against God, and God cast him out with his followers from heaven. He hates God and all that love God. Seeing our first parents, God's chosen creatures, happy in the garden of paradise, he tempted them by lies and deceits to disobey God, and thereby to defile their beautiful souls by the slimy guilt of mortal sin; his further cunningly concealed purpose being, to involve the whole human race in spiritual death. And it is easy to see how woefully well he has succeeded, and how widespread the havoc is, that he has caused. The voice of God which we hear echoing through the church, warns us to beware of him, that he is the prince of this world, the leader of the fallen angels who are spirits of wickedness, that he goeth about like a roaring lion seeking whom he may devour, and that to battle against him we must put on the whole armour of God—truth, justice, fortitude, faith, watchfulness, prayer, self-denial, or otherwise we shall be defeated. The church acknowledges this arch-enemy's great power, not only by her teaching but likewise by her prayers and ceremonies. In blessing churches, chalices, sacred Chrism, the Holy oils for the administration of the sacraments, the Holy Water, and other inanimate objects for sacred uses, the evil spirit is commanded to depart; the Christian ceremonial implying thereby, that all creation, since the fall, has been under blemish and enslaved by the powers of evil (Romans 8:21). In administering baptism, the priest commands the unclean spirit to go out of the person to be baptized, and to give place to the Holy Ghost the Paraclete, who is about to enter into and possess the soul of the Christian. The person receiving baptism, in like manner, says on his part: I renounce the Devil; I renounce his works; I renounce his pomps. The Holy Scriptures in several places tell us that Christ cast out devils (St. Luke 4:36); that He cast out a deaf and dumb spirit, and commanded him not to return any more into the person he possessed (St. Mark 9:24); that all that were possessed of devils were brought to Christ to be dispossessed of them (St Mark 1:32); that at the command of Christ, the devils went out from many, saying that He was the Son of God (St. Luke 4:41). The Scriptures tell us also, that Christ gave power to his Apostles to cast out devils in His name (St. Luke 10:17. St. Matthew 10:1).

WHERE GOD IS DENIED, THERE THE DEVIL HAS POWER.

No doubt the power of the devil was greatest before the coming of Christ, for it was to destroy the devil and his works that Christ came. The unlimited power of the devil among pagans, and among so-called Christians, who deny the faith and miracles of Christ, and give themselves up to the diablerie of spirit rapping, table turning, and the dark mysteries of the tripod, is no other than the result of their idolatry, whereby they acknowledge that there is no God but Satan, and that not God but Satan can do signs and wonders, and that to Satan alone belongs the knowledge of the future, and the holding of the destiny of mankind in his hands. From this source altogether came the bad morals and dark crimes of the pagans, who knew not God (1 Thess. 4:5), who would not have God in their knowledge (Romans 1:28), who changed the glory of the incorruptible God into the likeness of the image of corruptible man (Romans 1:23), who worshipped and served the

creature rather than the Creator (Romans 1:25).
Wherefore God delivered them up to a reprobate
sense, to do things unlawful and shameful (Romans
1:26); to idolatry, witchcraft, fornication, murder,
and the like, that exclude from the kingdom of God,
and that are worthy of death (Gal. 5:21). We are
amazed at the power of Satan, who by the Egyptian
magicians, changed a rod into a serpent, and changed
the rivers of Egypt into blood (Exodus 7). No less
amazing is the power of Satan, as seen in the divin-
ing woman of Endor, whom the wicked Saul, abandoned by God, called to his aid, to bring up the
Ghost of Samuel before him (1 Kings 28:7). The
Acts of the Apostles tell us of a certain man named
Simon, who had great power as a magician, but
whose heart was not right before God (Acts 8); and
that the evil spirit leaped upon, wounded, and
tore, certain Jewish exorcists, who attempted to cast
him out, which Christ alone and his apostles could do
(Acts 19:13). Satan has great power, but it is only
over pagans and bad Christians who acknowledge
Satan, and take him for their God.

"BRING IN THE PRIESTS OF THE CHURCH."

St. James 5:14.

In answer to a sick call from Hickory Branch, in
Chariton County, I took the evening train from
Chillicothe for Brookfield, twenty-six miles distant.
There I was met by a man on horseback, who was lead-
ing a horse already saddled and bridled for me. I set

out with my guide.   We rode on, through the hours
of the night, a journey of eighteen miles, in a south-
easterly direction, across the several branches of
Yellow Creek, through the timber and over the
prairies, of Linn and Chariton counties, until
we came to the Mulholland Place—the residence of James Mulholland— a whilom railroad
contractor, and at this time a well-to-do farmer, ad-
vantageously settled on some of the most productive
land in fertile Missouri.   Received politely and with
welcome, I entered the elegant country mansion, and
was led without delay into the presence of the most
beloved member of the family—a young lady, faint
and almost lifeless, over whose features and emaciated
form a pallor like death had spread.   There was no
time to be lost.   The immortal soul, the pearl of
value beyond price, was to be prepared to worthily
meet with God.   I reverently administered the last
sacraments, which the angelic child received with
tenderest faith and devotion.   Then leaving her
awhile to commune in thought with God and his angels, I retired to another room to converse with the
child's mother.   The anxious mother told me that
their family physician, having consulted with other
physicians in that part of the country, had concluded
that nothing in their power remained to be
done; and that the final event, against which there
seemed no hope, had to be waited for in patience.
But, she added, there is an old man, living

in this county, who has the reputation of having cured many by some charms or supernatural agency that he has, and he has sent me word, that if I would send for him he would cure my Catherine. Reverend Father, what do you advise me to do; shall I send for him? My Catherine, my beloved child, is very dear to me, and she is very low. Oh, no, no, no, said I, your dear child belongs to God, she is God's chosen one, she puts her trust in God, who is able to keep her, and restore her to health if such be His Holy and Adorable Will. She has received the Last Sacraments, and is willing and ready to go with her Heavenly Bridegroom, to the Heavenly Marriage Feast, if He be pleased to call her now. O thrice happy Christian mother, how great the honor, the joy, and the consolation that is yours, to have so saintly a child; one who now, after Holy Communion, is in happy intercourse with God, in the midst of his angels and saints, and very likely pleading and interceding for you. God alone is her portion and her inheritance, and she will have no other. She is not afraid of her future. Nor does she care to know, what she entirely trusts to her God, whether she shall live or die. She knows that her Redeemer knows what is best for her, and therefore she puts her trust entirely in Him, and in Him only. Away, then, with all snares and deceits of the devil—the lying spirit from the beginning—in whom no dependence is to be placed. Nor is your child's case in any sense hopeless. She yet has life. Looking along the ways of God's providence "who ordereth all things in mercy," I advise you in God's name, and for her sake, to take her to St. Louis, and put her under the care of the eminent physicians you will find there—Doctor Linton and Doctor Gregory—the most renowned, successful and tender-hearted physicians to be found in this whole country. Your daughter is as holy and dear to God as young Tobias was. Be you to her a true Christian Mother; an Archangel Raphael to your heavenly protege; and I venture to say, as I give you and her my blessing, that God will bless you both on your journey, and that He will bring you both home safe, and that she will recover her health.

AFFLICTIONS AND CONSOLATIONS.

By slow and easy stages, the mother with her daughter in charge, reached St. Louis; where, having called in and consulted Doctor Linton and Doctor Gregory, the conclusion was reached, that the child could not be cured unless by a most difficult and dangerous surgical operation, to survive which in her feeble condition was as one chance in a hundred. Between certain death and a mere chance for life, there was no middle ground. The chance for life was chosen by mother and daughter. Again the saintly sufferer prepared herself by the most devout reception of her Divine Lord in the most adorable sacrament of the Eucharist. Submitting herself to the Divine Will of Him who loved her most, and in whom she trusted, the tedious and painful operation was performed. A little flickering, struggling ray of life was left, scarcely perceptible, ebbing ever and anon, this way and that, and oh, how breathlessly guarded by the pulseless mother, whose life, too, was in the issue. Oh precious life, stay with us, and spare the poor mother's heart. Oh Heavenly giver of life, spare thy loving children who have put their trust in Thee. The humble prayers, and they were many that were offered for her, were heard. Slowly life returned, then increasing strength and afterwards health. It was another such merciful act from the tender heart of Jesus, as when through compassion for disconsolate friends, He took hold of the hand of the deceased daughter of Jairus, and said to her: "Young maiden, I say to thee, arise," and she rose up and walked, and was given back to her parents (St. Mark 5:41). Catherine, who was mourned as one dead, was restored to life again, and went home with her mother rejoicing. These events, which are but a part of this narrative, took place in the year 1862.

CONSOLATIONS AND AFFLICTIONS.

On the 12th day of March, 1863, there was great rejoicing at the house of James Mulholland, in Chariton County. It was the marriage day of his beloved daughter Catherine, to James Shaughnessy—a very worthy young man of that county. And on

the 10th of February of the year following, there
was another such rejoicing; it was the baptismal day
of Elizabeth, the first born of these virtuous parents.
But clouds will come and overspread the brightest
sky. The young mother, from sudden fright and
alarm for the safety of her child, lost her reason.
For weeks she lay writhing in madness of the most
violent and uncontrollable kind. Again, as on the
several previous occasions of alternating joy and sorrow, the pastor was anxiously sought. I found the
dear child in one continuing paroxysm, ever requiring strong and tender hands to keep her in bed, and
to prevent her from biting and lacerating her arms
and shoulders, and from doing like injury to those
around her. Every article of movable furniture had
to be put out of the room, to prevent what she had
frequently attempted—jumping for and seizing whatever appurtenance she could see, wherewith to do
violence to herself or those around her, who, in their
sore pity had to watch at her bedside—a post of duty
at which she would consentingly suffer no one but a
favorite sister and her pastor. Again God's mercy
was earnestly besought by the Holy Mass and prayers
to restore the afflicted one to reason and health. And
again, the same temptations as before had to be encountered and resisted. The Old Man, professing to
have wonderful powers, but not from God, was
again heard of. This time he sent word not only to
the loving parents, but also and especially to the sor-

row-stricken husband, to be allowed to restore the
lady to health, which he promised to do if invited to
make use of his profession. At this crisis I re-
doubled my prayers as well as my entreaties. To
all I replied, that God's merciful and providential
ways alone had to be followed, invoked, and con-
fided in; and that no power but God's should be
sought or admitted in the affairs and destinies of that
truly Christian family. My exhortations and entreaties were listened to, and the hopes that centered
in God were not disappointed. Again health was restored, to the great joy of the Lady and her dear
friends. Again the dear little infant, that had strug-
gled for life, without the care of its mother, throughout the long storm, was received lovingly into the
care and fondness of the maternal bosom. It was
all caused by the unfortunate remark of a friendly,
but unwitted neighboring woman, who had said to
the mother after the infant's birth, its limbs were de-
formed, which was by no means the case. The cruel
remark had crazed the mother.

THE HAUNTED HOUSE.

It was now the autumn of 1864, the fourth year
of the war. The wildest terror overspread North
Missouri. Bushwhackers and guerillas were everywhere. Murders, robberies, and burnings were of
daily occurrence. And above all places, Chariton
County was the theatre of dark and atrocious crimes.
The Mulhollands and Shaughnessys abandoned their

homes, and fled for greater safety; some to Brookfield, some to St. Catherine's, and some to Center
Point. I noticed that these terror-stricken refugees
were regular attendants at Mass at Brookfield, on the
days appointed for Mass there—the fourth Sunday
of each month. One of the Shaughnessys, with his
family, occupied temporarily the vacant residence of
Squire Sportsman, close by the railroad, on the east
bank of East Yellow Creek, near Center Point; the
Squire having fled from the place and gone to Cali-
fornia at the beginning of the war. The Squire's
log mansion, the first built and longest inhabited
house in that part of the country, did not, as the
event proved, entirely suit the tastes of the new-
comers. No doubt it was so, because they were the
first to make the sign of the cross within its walls,
and to shake the holy water over its foundations. We
have heard of a strong city long ago, the walls of
which fell down, when assaulted by the prayers of
the servants of the Lord. And if the Missouri
Squire's log castle did not come down so readily
in a tumble, it was, as we shall see, because there
was in it unbeknown, "a strong armed man determined to keep his court." (St. Luke 11:21.)

On a Sunday after Mass at Brookfield, the Center Point Shaughnessys, attended by many of their
neighbors, called on me for consultation and advice. They said that since they had occupied the
Sportsman residence, they were subjected to terrors

of an extraordinary kind. That, commencing with sunset, and between that time and nightfall, loud knocking noises were frequently heard, within, outside, and under the floor of the house; and that these noises were so strange and unusual as to cause the dogs to howl, and the fowls to fly off their roost. They said also, that at these times, a man, strange and unknown to them, was usually seen walking outside, around the house, and from the house to an outside kitchen, close by the end of the house; and that upon search being made for him, he was nowhere to be found. Furthermore they averred, that during the hours of the night, the beds, doors, windows, and furniture of the house rattled and shook, and that the house itself seemed to move and sway on its side. Yet, when they arose and lighted the lights, the commotion usually had ceased, and nothing seemed disturbed, or out of order. The strange visitor that was so often seen around the premises, was noticed by persons outside the house, to pass out directly from the door; and yet, upon inquiry, the inmates had no knowledge of the presence of such a person amongst them. These facts were testified to before me, by persons living in the house, and by out-siders —catholic and non-catholic—who had gone to the house through curiosity, or in order to find out the imposition, if such had been practised there. Several testified, and these were chiefly men, that when they heard the noises, and the hammering on the floor under their feet, where there was neither space nor cellar that they hastened out of the house, and could not be induced to return there. Those that I examined were persons above suspicion of collusion or deceit; and I found that were I to continue the examination, as many as forty could be produced, witnesses of these facts, and present when they had occurred. There was nothing left for me but to conclude, that these terrified people were convinced, as I was by their testimony, that the case was one of supernatural agency.

BEELZEBUB CAST OUT.

Mr. Shaughnessy and his wife besought me to go with them to their house, to stay with them there that night, and to say Mass for them there the next morning. For this I did not feel prepared, especially as I was convinced that I would have to meet there a vexing evil spirit. I replied that I was not ready just then, but that I would soon appoint a time to be with them, of which I would give them due previous notice, so that all could prepare to assist at Mass and receive the sacraments. Mindful of the rebuke of Our Lord to his Apostles, who, although having received power from Him to cast out devils in His name (St. Luke 10:17), were nevertheless unable to do so, for want of certain necessary virtues in themselves (St. Mark 9:28); I thought it to be my duty, and in a measure necessary for my safety, to make a spiritual retreat of some days in prayer and fasting. Accordingly I entered into retreat. But scarcely had I begun, when I was obliged to go on a sick call, east of Center Point, in the direction of Macon City. Having attended the sick call, it was in order for me to insist with myself on keeping a good rule I had made for my better guidance; never to delay unnecessarily at a place from home, after my duty there had been complied with. So, taking the first train that came along, which happened to be a freight train, I was soon on my way westward, towards Brookfield and Chillicothe. Naturally my mind reverted to the Sportsman Log House, now become a place of grave concern to me, towards which the train was hurrying, and close by which the train was to stop, at a water tank at East Yellow Creek. I remembered, from my many former journeys on freight trains over the same place, that with the engine at a stop, taking water at the tank, the caboose, always the hindmost car of the train, rested so near the Sportsman house, as to be within a few feet of it, across the fence, by the side of the track. Accordingly, as the train approached the place, I prepared myself for the opportunity by holding the ritual open in my hand, with the words of Exorcism on the page before me. Going out on the rear platform of the car, as it came to a stop at the spot, I read from the ritual, the command to the evil spirit in possession of that place, in the name and by the power of Jesus, to depart therefrom, and never again to return thereto. Soon again the train was on its way. I was convinced that the work I had to do was done. In about a week I made inquiries whether my presence would be needed at Mr. Shaughnessy's, at East Yellow Creek. The word came back that the causes for my going there no longer existed.

"FROM AN ILL END DELIVER HIM, O LORD."
Litany for a soul departing.

Some time afterwards I was again called to Mr. Shaughnessy's, of East Yellow Creek, but upon another business—to attend a sick man, who lived in a little house adjoining, and who was resident there when Mr. Shaughnessy took possession of the place. Arrived at East Yellow Creek, I entered the dark but not otherwise altogether uninviting little abode. I found the patient, an old, decrepit little man, very sick, and almost in immediate danger of death. I explained to him the mercies of our Heavenly Redeemer, the Son of God, who died on the cross to save sinners, and who was ever willing to pardon sinners if they would but repent of their sins, and return to Him with sorrow for what they had done, and with love for Him in their hearts. For hours I stayed by the side of this poor sick man, leaving him betimes to himself to think of himself and his God; then again returning to encourage him with suggestions and promises by renewed hopes and consolations. Through God's all-powerful and all-merciful grace, my prayers and exhortations were not in vain. The poor dying man put his hope and trust in God, and continually prayed to God for mercy and pardon. Seeing his good dispositions I administered the Last Sacraments to him, according to his great needs. Then, helping him to make his thanksgiving, and to renew his acts of Faith, Hope and Love for God; also recommending to him to invoke the patronage and intercession of the Blessed Mother of God, and that of St. Joseph, I imparted to him the Last Blessing and Plenary Indulgence for the dying. Reluctant to leave the dark little cabin that was now a sacred place, I fondly cast a last look on the paling features of the poor man that was so dear to me. Then with a fast throbbing heart, and with eyes suffused with tears, I left that ever memorable humble scene, on which God had so mercifully cast the light of His Heavenly Countenance. Shortly afterwards, the soul of the dying Christian departed. His mortal remains were borne by loving hands, and laid side by side with the saintly dead, in the secluded little cemetery, set apart in that neighborhood for Catholic burial, in a grove on the hillside, on the verge of the prairie. It was whispered among the mourners, as they departed from the sacred place; that he who was that day laid to rest, had been once a noted magician in Chariton County; and that the extraordinary occurrances at Squire Sportsman's of late, must have resulted from his presence as a dweller there.

The foregoing narrative, prepared by me in manuscript, word for word as it appears in print, was sent by me to Mr. James Shaughnessy, a surviving witness, most intimately connected with these events; my purpose for writing to him having been, to test the reliability of my memory of the facts I have recited. His answer to me is as follows: "Padgett, Chariton County, Missouri, April 12, 1892. Right Reverend John J. Hogan; Bishop of Kansas City; Administrator of St. Joseph. Right Reverend and Dear Bishop: I received the manuscript you kindly sent me. I find it correct as I remember it. The old man who used to set charms was named David Condon. It was my brother John who lived at Sportsman's. The ghost story is true as you related it. We thank you for your kind remembrance of my wife's parents— Mr. and Mrs. Mulholland; and we are greatly pleased that you have not forgotten any of us. My wife and daughter, the subjects of your narrative, send you their most respectful filial obedience and regards. Kneeling, we ask your blessing, and will ever pray for your welfare. Your humble servant, Jas. Shaughnessy."

CHAPTER XX

ST. BRIDGET'S CHURCH, PEABODY.

THE gradual increase of Catholic settlers along the line of the Hannibal & St. Joseph Rail-Road, and between the Chariton River and Yellow Creek in the counties of Linn, Macon and Chariton, made it a matter of duty for me to build a church for them. There was much difficulty in selecting a site to suit all who had preferences in the matter. Some wished the church built at Bucklin, some at Peabody, and some at Stockton. I selected the place that seemed most central. That place was Peabody, which was so called from its owner, Colonel Peabody, who fought with Colonel Mulligan on the Union side at Lexington, and was killed soon afterwards at the battle of Shiloh. A small, neat, convenient frame church was built, at a cost of about eight hundred dollars, which was subscribed and paid without delay. It was dedicated to Saint Bridget, Patroness of Ireland, and was well attended by the congregation that built it, who were pious, honest, virtuous people. Some families travelling by in their wagons camped near the church at night, and in the morning, when leaving the place, neglected to extinguish their camp fires. The wind rose and blew the smouldering fire against the building, which was soon ablaze and burned to the ground. There was no insurance. I loved the little building for its name, its devotional seclusion, and the piety of the people who attended it. Peabody is now called Lingo. Stockton has changed its name to New Cambria. New Cambria and Bucklin have each a Catholic church, and there is a probability that St. Bridget's will be soon rebuilt. St. Bridget's was built in 1865 and burned in 1866.

GREATER THAN A CENTURION.

In the beginning of October, 1866, a man somewhat past middle life, of dignified manner and pleasing address, called on me at my residence in Chillicothe, to ask me to baptize his child, which he said he had brought from his home forty miles distant in Carroll County. Looking through the window, I saw at the gate, a pair of horses harnessed to a barouche, in which two ladies sat, one of them holding a child in her arms. I told the gentleman to take the child to the church, and that I would be there with him in a few minutes. At the church, prepared to proceed with the baptism, I called for the Sponsors. A lady stepped forward to be God-mother. The gentleman, a little disconcerted in manner and bowing politely, apologized for his unreadiness to present a God-father, for the reason that he was a stranger, lately moved into Missouri, and therefore unacquainted with any person who could oblige him in the matter, or of whom he would ask so great a favor. But, said he, and he bowed still more profoundly, "Reverend Father if you would be pleased to do me the great favor and honor of being God-father for my child I would ever remember it for you with sincerest affection and gratitude." ·I could not but grant the request in so far as was in my power to do, although it was not clear to my mind that the baptizer and God-father should not be different persons. Nevertheless, in the emergency I proceded with the baptism. The baptism administered, I made entry in the baptismal register as follows: "Chillicothe, October 4, 1866; I baptized James, born May 15, 1866; son of James Shields and Mary Carr, his wife: Sponsors, Rev. John Hogan and Mary D. Hilton. John Hogan "Some days afterwards I learned that my visitor, was no other than Major General James Shields of the United States Army, the great patriot, statesman, and soldier, who, for thirty years, having served his country faithfully, on the Bench, the Forum, the Senate Chamber, and the Battle Field, had now retired from public life, to spend the remainder of his years in the tranquil enjoyment of his rural home in the pleasant prairies of North Missouri. That he was as faithful a member of the Catholic Church, which he loved and revered with all his soul, as he was a loyal and loving citizen of the Great Republic, for which he bled almost to

death on many a battle field, the foregoing journey
to procure baptism for his child is full attest.

EPISCOPAL VISITATION.

The first visit of a bishop to these new missions
took place on Ascension Thursday, 1860, and was
made, as hereinbefore stated, by the Right Reverend
James O'Gorman, D. D., Vicar Apostolic of Nebraska, who administered Confirmation at Chillicothe.
The long wished for and many times requested visit
of the Most Reverend Peter Richard Kenrick, D.D.,
Archbishop of St. Louis, the Ordinary of the diocese,
was at last made, on December the 8th, 1866, when
he administered Confirmation at Brookfield, and on
December the 9th, 1866, when he administered Confirmation at Chillicothe. It was while at Chillicothe
on this date and occasion, that he received the happy
news by telegraph from Washington, that the Missouri Test Oath was declared unconstitutional by the
United States Supreme Court. The names of those
Confirmed at Brookfield and Chillicothe are as follows:

CONFIRMED AT BROOKFIELD.

James Riley,	Thomas Dixon,
Catherine Mary Cairy,	John Doolan,
Timothy Devine,	Patrick Burns,
Sarah Riley,	Margaret Doolan,
Augustine Tooey,	Thomas Duffy,
James Riley,	John Moore,
James Tooey,	John McGowan,
Mary Donnelly,	Thomas Reilly,

Rosanna Reily, Catherine Ryan,
Thomas Daly, James McGowan,
Margaret Moore, James McGreale,
Maurice Bresnahan, Thomas O'Neal,
John Doyle, Elizabeth Burns,
Patrick Curten, James Dillon,
Thomas Tooey, Simon Kennedy,
Patrick Tooey, Michael Reily,
James Tooey, Edward Doolan,
Catherine Shea, Zelia Stephens,
Margaret Brown, Anne Mulholland,
Ellen Collins, James Doyle,
Daniel Bresnahan, Mary Jane Kennedy,
Sarah Frances Campbell, William Kirk,
Magdalena Yagel, Josephine Donnelly,
Mary Anne Kerns, Catherine Donnelly,
Viola Logsdon, Julia Reily,
Sara Laura Logsdon, Mary Anne Daly,
Michael Quealy, Bridget Gavan,

CONFIRMED AT CHILLICOTHE.

Octavius Lamarce Owen Padden,
Br'g't Anastasia Roach, Michael Slattery,
Mary Agnes Roach, Joh'na Mary McGrogan,
Margaret Mullens, Margaret Cunningham,
Ellen Holland, Mary Kennedy,
Susan M'Bride, William Kelly,
Bridget Walsh, Margaret King,
Catherine Walsh, Ellen Galvin,
Mary Tierney, Mary Ellen Reily,

Ellen Shea,	Johanna Slattery,
Mary Galvin,	Mary Agnes Hurst,
Mary Ellen Farrell,	Margaret McGrogan,
Mary Lloyd,	Mary Salome Labri,
Margaret Russel,	James Holland,
Mary Murray,	John McNicholas,
Mary Catherine Dunn,	Alduff James Labri,
Thomas Keenan,	Stephen Brown,
Michael Galvin,	James Fahy,
Bridget Cunningham,	William Hurst,
Peter Sauveur Demaree,	Mary Teresa Markey,
Thomas Kennedy,	William Morritz,
Martin Walsh,	Patrick Carter,
John Walsh,	Alice Kelly,
Mary Salome Lamaree,	Margaret Slattery,

FOR BETTER FOR WORSE.

"From this day forward, for better for worse, for richer for poorer, in sickness and in health, till death do us part." Such are the strong, tender and solemn words, spoken by the heart more than by the lips, when young man and maiden, kneeling for the nuptial blessing before the altar of God, enter upon that new career which the Creator instituted and blessed in the marriage of our First Parents. The marriage ceremony is a solemn religious act, a holy sacrament of divine institution; from which, if its religiousness or the awful sacredness of its engagement, be banished or lost sight of, but little happiness can be assured to those entering upon it, whose irreli-

gious principles and unchecked passions would make
it for themselves and for civil society, not a haven of
peace or a storehouse of blessings, but a wild un-
governable storm of malediction and tribulation.
Marriage vows are for the most part, thank God,
faithfully and sacredly kept; and this heaven-given
grace with its corresponding happy influence would
be more general, were the conjugal state generally
regarded as it should be, in the seriousness, responsibility, sanctity, and dignity, with which religion
inspires it. The good reason for the abiding fidelity
and sacred respect for marriage, is found paramount
in the wisdom and firmness of the church of God,
which everywhere throughout the world, undeterred
by the clamor of ungodly people and their passions,
holds civil society to the basis of Christian marriage
and does not permit wandering eyes and wayward
hearts—never, alas, too right before God—to stray
away on the wings of forbidden love, or to ex-
change for the destroying phantom of the passions,
the pure joy of home and the affections born of family ties that have their origin in modesty sanctified by
religion. In this connection I have to record an
unfaithful marriage, thank God, the only one of
the kind that came to my knowledge, in my eleven
years missionary experience in North Missouri. It
is impossible for me in this recital, to repress the
tears that come unbidden to my eyes, when I think
of the woes of a deserted family in their darkest

hour of poverty, sickness, and death.

SEEK NOT YOUR FUTURE TO KNOW.

Julia, Lizzie, William, Edward, and Joseph, fond brothers and sisters from two to ten years of age, were the loving children of parents, one of whom was a professed unbeliever in religion, and the other—the mother—a pious exemplary Catholic. Until sickness came on, the necessaries of life were provided for the family by the father, who was a mechanic. But the dark hour for the family came when the mother fell sick. She was ailing, or rather failing in health for over a year. Finally she had to retire to her bed, unable to work any longer. With this was conveyed by the weeping children to the neighbors, the further bad news, that their father had gone away from them some days before, they did not know whereto, that they were hungry and had nothing to eat, and that their Mamma was very sick in bed and had no one to attend her. It was time for the neighbors to step in. They found the mother, to their pity and grief, in abject poverty, suffering from virulent cancer in its advanced stages, and without medical aid. It was useless to look for the father. He had collected his earnings and gone away. And report, true or false, did not fail to connect his departure with that of another, who was more youthful and in better health than the poor dying mother. Thenceforward the mother and children wanted for nothing that tender care and loving kindness could bestow on them. It was to great purpose to humanity that Jesus Christ our Redeemer the Eternal Son of God condescended to become man, and to be poor, outcast and despised in this world. He has said to us that He is our brother, that we are all His brethren and of each other, and that, whatever we do to help the sick, needy, or disconsolate, we do it to Him and for His sake, and that He will reward us, as His own, and with eternal life. Therefore the Christian for Christ's sake, will always love the poor, and help them, and bend down his ear to them, to hear their moans and plaints. The sick lady and her dear little children, no longer stood in need of a husband or a father. Christ the father of the poor and the needy had provided for all this, and had made it a joyful act to cleanse the ulcerous sores and be a father to the orphan. After almost a whole year of tenderest care from the charitable ladies of the neighborhood, who paid the house rent, tended the children, waited on the sick mother, and kept the house clean, bright and warm, the Father of the poor, who reigns gloriously in heaven, took the dying Christian mother to Himself. Her trials and struggles were over. There were none but the five little children to be provided for. The pious Christian ladies kept them still in their mother's home, and stayed with them occasionally or by turns for company, and to help them in their wants. Soon new dresses and nice clothing, hats and coats, and cloaks and bonnets, were provided for the little ones. They were all invited, and many other children besides of their age and acquaintance, to spend a day at the priest's house. The happy company soon came together, and there never was a merrier, gayer, or brighter. They feasted and played the whole day. In and around the house, along the grassy lawn, and under the shady trees, their plays went on, until towards evening, when several ladies and gentlemen arrived in wagons and buggies, and joined in the play. One by one, the dear little children of the loving mother who had gone to heaven, were coaxed and invited by these ladies and gentlemen to ride with them in their wagons and buggies. The invitations were joyfully accepted. They rode away, some this way and some that, some in opposite directions, never thinking or suspecting the purpose. Their home was broken up. Their father gone. Their mother in Heaven. New homes had been provided for them. They were henceforward to live with strangers, though good and kind. Never again were their loving hearts to beat, as fond brothers and sisters together in their own home. My heart was sore with grief for the dear little children whom I had learned to love as my own. But how could I have told them, that they were to be separated, and that that meeting, they had been invited to, was to be their final parting. It is not good for us to seek or crave to know our future.

We are in the hands of God, who knows what is best for us. His Providence will protect us. His love will lead us on in the right way.

MY CHRISTMAS PRESENT.

At Brookfield, where the best people in the world live, there was a widow, who, though not possessed of "two mites that make a farthing," had nevertheless a flock of turkeys, the largest of which she selected for her pastor for Christmas. Christmas coming on; twig in hand, she marched her bird, as tall as an ostrich, to the railway depot for shipment. The depot master, informed of the consignee whom he knew well, with admirable humor, tied a string around the turkey's neck, to which was fastened a piece of pasteboard, on which was conspicuously written: "FATHER HOGAN, CHILLICOTHE." The train boys as usual welcomed Father Hogan aboard their caboose car, and greatly enjoyed his company to Chillicothe. On the way, not wishing to lose the opportunity for the conversion of an incorrigible one of their companions, they made him go on his knees and make a general confession, and a promise of amendment of his bad behavior, to His Reverence with the tag on his breast; who, the while, listened with dignified composure, and without emotion at the prodigal's recital. The boys stopped their train before my door, and marched my namesake into my presence. Out of reverence for the "Widow's Mite," there were two Father Hogans at the priest's house in Chillicothe, for many a day.

CHAPTER XXI.

CLIMATE.

MISSOURI, the center of a large level continent, remote from the shelter of mountain ranges and the influence of sea breezes, is subject to varying temperature, according as the winds that blow over it, come from warmer or colder climates. Generally the climate is mild, balmy, and pleasant. Occasionally extremes of heat and cold of short duration, alternate with the prevailing moderate weather. The frosty breezes following close on the winter solstice, sometimes register twenty degrees below zero. Also, in the calm, following the summer solstice, ninety degrees in the shade, and one hundred and twenty in the sun, mark the other limit. These extremes, however, seldom continue long, as more temperate weather returns with change of the veering wind.

INDIAN SUMMER.

No climate is more delightful than the Missouri Indian Summer, usually ranging from the middle of September to the middle of November, when the blue azure sky, aglow with warm sunlight, appears mellowed and tinted by the calm autumnal haze that permeates the whole firmament, near and far away, in the immeasurable zenith and the limitless horizon. Then in the noiseless melody of nature, the little birds seem to forget their songs, the waving boughs of the forest lose their swaying motion, and the babbling brooks cease their clamor; so intent does creation seem, to enjoy its siesta, during which the human mind yields much of its turmoil to the the happy hour of prevailing restfulness.

DECEIVINGLY BEAUTIFUL.

But these soft hazy hours are not to be trusted too much, especially when with the waning year, they take wings and vanish, before the bold advance of winter. The traveller on our prairies who would dream of unchanging sunshine in the latter days of November, would be apt to be rudely undeceived, as I often was in the guileless days of my youth now long since gone by. Once having left home, in a light summer suit, in the warm November sunshine, I was some hours afterwards, riding north-eastward on horseback, from a railway station near Chariton River, on a sick call, into Macon County. Suddenly in the north-western horizon, great masses of dark clouds began rising and rolling onward towards me. At once my trusted companion, the Indian Summer, fled, leaving me not a ray of its warmth or effulgence. The roaring winds and rushing clouds were at once upon me, pelting me unmercifully with their missiles of hail and snow. There was no shelter near. I had to keep onward in my course, chastised almost to death by the storm. My left side, face, and neck, were exposed for hours to the fury of the elements; with the painful result, that my left ear was frozen, and thereby deprived of hearing; a sad reminder to a foolish young man, of his too great confidence in the sunny smiles of the Indian Summer's bewitching twilight.

DECEIVED AGAIN.

Some years afterwards, another such experience of the tempting November sunshine, nearly cost me my life. It was in a snow storm, in an uncovered wagon, on the high prairies of Caldwell County, while travelling northward, and at night, towards Hamilton, from Shoal Creek; where I had been called from Chillicothe, to attend in his dying hours, a member of my flock, living in that remote region, and isolated from church and altar. The thick pelting storm from the north, struck me straight in the face, and filled my mouth, eyes, and ears with snow, and likewise filled the roads; so that almost sightless and trackless, and clad in thin summer raiment, I had to contend for life, for hours, in the dark night, on the wind-swept prairie, before gaining a place of shelter.

AGAIN DECEIVED AND TURNED ROBBER.

The third such experience of delusive November sunshine, caused me to degrade myself to sheep stealer, or, to what is baser still—sheep skin stealer. It was likewise in Caldwell County, on the elevated prairie between Hamilton and Cameron, and at the midnight hour, which is usually the thief's chosen time. I was burthened with but a light summer coat, in which I had set out from home, while the sun was bright and warm, and with never a cloud on the firmament. It did not matter much that I had to travel at night, for I was still young, and on a fleet, elegant horse. As had happened to me before in November, when the sun went down, big clouds came up, and with these came hail, frost and snow. I was passing by a farm house, near which was a cattle shed, on the roof of which I saw a sheep skin. I was indeed very cold, but not quite so benumbed as to be unable to execute the light-fingered job, that transferred the sheep skin from its perch to my shoulders, and with the woolly side out for fashion's sake. I rode on comfortably during the remainder of the night. But when morning dawned, I began to see, and without much examination of conscience, that I had become a different man; and that the change I had undergone, was altogether for worse. The side of the skin that wasn't woolly, was the one that I had put inwards on me; and as it was fresh from the animal that owned it, its lubricating qualities played sad havoc with the decency of my rusty clerical raiment. I felt all the horrors of my immundicity—a thief dyed in the wool, a veritable wolf in sheep's clothing. My remorse was so great, that on my return journey, I called on the man I had robbed, and fully confessed my crime to him. Good man that he was, he freely forgave me, and joined with me in a hearty laugh at my thieving adventure. In the mean time, I had bought a new coat, to present myself in, as a decent Christian.

BLUSTERING MID-WINTER.

Dark, blustering mid-winter in its undisguised severity, on the honest principle of forewarned forearmed, is far less dangerous to health, than flattering autumnal sunshine. An equipment of over shoes, buck skin gloves, fur cap with ear lapels, and heavy overcoat, makes a man ironclad, against the assaults of winter. Thus clad I made many a winter's journey, and with exhilirating effect, of great benefit to my health. On a very cold day, the 1st of January, 1860, which was the coldest day in my memory in Missouri, the thermometer being twenty-eight degrees below zero, I travelled comfortably and with safety in an open sleigh, twelve miles from Chillicothe to Medicine Creek and return, to baptize a child in danger of death. The sky was clear azure blue, and the atmosphere through which the feeble sunlight scarcely passed, was piercingly cold. But good heavy clothing and warm lap robes kept me comfortable in the sleigh. The baptism was as follows, as of record, in the Chillicothe baptismal register. "1860, January 1, I baptized Ellen, born Dec. 25th, 1859, daughter of William Doyle and Hannah Walsh, his wife. Sponsors,

John Doyle, and Sarah Reilly.   John Hogan."

THE DISAPPOINTED WEDDING.

On Tuesday morning, January 22d, 1861, after a weary night of travel on a slow train, from Mexico, by way of Macon City to Chillicothe, I set out in a two-horse sleigh, on a journey that was to take the whole day, to go to the neighborhood of Carrollton, in Carroll County, to marry a couple there that evening.   The friends of the parties to be married, who had called on me some time previous, to make arrangements with me for the solemn occasion appointed by them for that day, besought me to make the journey to Carroll County on the day previous to that set for the marriage, so as to prevent disappointment that might otherwise possibly occur.   I could not accede to their wishes, as I had to keep my regular appointment for Mass at Mexico on the third Sunday of the month, after which I would necessarily have to wait for the first north-bound train, which, according to its schedule time, was not to pass Mexico until Monday noon, and by connection with another train at Macon City, was not to reach Chillicothe until fifteen minutes before two o'clock on Tuesday morning.   The journey by train was made throughout on schedule time.   After my arrival at Chillicothe I took a short rest.   Soon after daylight, I set out in a two horse sleigh with a driver, for Carroll County.   The weather was intensely cold. Deep snow had covered the ground, and it was

freezing hard through an azure blue atmosphere,
with scarcely perceptible sunshine.   We crossed
Grand River on the ice, and without risk, as
heavily loaded teams had made the frozen river a
travelled roadway.   Afterwards, driving over the
level alluvial lands along the west bank of Shoal
Creek, between it and Utica, in going over the slip-
pery surface of a frozen lake, from which the wind
had blown away the snow, we noticed that one of the
horses was not properly shod for the journey, as he
was constantly slipping on the glassy surface. Soon,
in spite of all we could do to prevent the accident,
that poor horse fell down heavily, and was with great
difficulty got to stand up and trust to his feet again.
That was the first accident, and delay in "the haste
to the wedding" which had now or never to be played
to time.   After a little, the horses were on the move
once more, slowly at first, then gradually limbering
to the task, a high and steady rate of speed was
gained.   Having passed Shoal Creek and the frozen
lagoons along its banks, the rolling prairies through
the Blue Mound country and over the borders into
Carroll County were passed in speed and safety, and
there seemed no doubt whatever that the marriage
rendezvous would be reached in good time.   But
disappointments will come anon to mar the fullest
hopes and cloud the brightest scenes.   Some miles
farther on, and within one hour's drive of the end of
the journey, when near Bogard's Mound, in crossing

a wooden bridge without parapets, that spanned a frozen stream, one of the horses affrighted by the loose, shaky planks under his feet, shied badly, and shoved the other horse sidelong over the bridge, with result that one horse and the sleigh were on the bridge, and the other horse was on his back on the ice below. Having scanned the situation we hastily unhitched the horse on the bridge from the sleigh, and tied him by the halter to a tree near by; then going to the relief of the horse that was down, we found him on his back, trembling and stunned, his four legs standing out from his body, straight upright. Nothing could induce him to rise, or to make an effort to do so. He suffered himself to be shoved and turned round and round on his back on the ice, his limbs seeming to grow stiffer all the while. At length, when he had rested himself well, and when the fright had left him, he seemed inclined to make efforts to rise. Then, some brambles placed along his sides and around him, he succeeded in rising, and getting on his feet again. Upon examination we found he was uninjured, though somewhat bruised and greatly frightened and stunned. It required considerable time to limber him, and get him ready for work, by rubbing his limbs, and relaxing them by exercise. Then the harness had to be re-adjusted and tied and knotted together. Afterwards, the horses were brought together, and hitched to their traces. The whole loss of time by the accident was fully three hours. Already night had set in. Six miles remained to be travelled, necessarily at a slow gait. The wedding hour had come and gone. And there was no courier near, to be sent forward in speed, to announce the completion of the journey with its reverses. At length we arrived, tired, weary and disheartened. The marriage feast had been partaken of. "The lights were fled, the garlands dead, the banquet hall deserted." The marriage party with the bride and bridegroom, had set out in sleighs towards Lexington to have the marriage duly solemnized there. I did my best. It was a great disappointment. But the causes were beyond my control. And now though more than thirty years have elapsed, my heart still beats with pity for them, for having had to go so far through the cold winter's night, for the performance of a sacred duty, the appointed minister of which was near at hand, even at their very doors, if they but knew of his approach. Other reasons, too, there are, why the sadness of that occasion, seems to be a never-ceasing one. The good and beautiful bride of that night, has long since been laid to rest in her quiet grave. And the worthy bridegroom, ever with bowed head, goes down the hill of life, silent and alone; seemingly with no purpose on earth, but to look forward to another marriage feast, and in a better world, where sorrow shall be no more, and all disappointment will have passed away.

"YOU MUST BE BORN AGAIN."

St. John 3:7

Weary and tired I endeavored to attend to the duty of reciting my Office and night prayers, in the comfortable but now cheerless house, which the disappointed wedding party had so recently deserted. To seek immediate rest, in my unnerved and over-fatigued condition, would be quite useless. I reposed quietly for a while in an easy chair. The venerable lady of the house, whose daughter was the bride, was too anxious for the safety of the wedding party, then toiling through the snow, to compose herself to sleep. She too, had lulled herself into a wakeful repose, on a rocking chair, before the smouldering embers in the fire-place. The lamps had been turned down to a dull shady gloom. Now and then we conversed a little in under tones, in keeping with the solitariness of the scene and the midnight hour, which a drowsy little timepiece on the mantel had just announced. What sounded like a feeble knock was heard at the door, but there were no voices or footfalls that we could hear. After a while, the faint knock was repeated, and with it a feeble voice asked for admission. The lady of the house arose and went to the door, which, after having listened warily awhile, she cautiously opened. A lady entered, wrapped in heavy winter robes, and bearing an infant sheltered in her bosom. She was attended by her husband, a middle-aged gentleman, likewise dressed in winter clothing, and of respectful demeanor. Having exchanged salutations with the lady of the house, with whom they were acquainted, they asked to be introduced to the priest, saying that they had brought their babe to be baptized, and had come at that late hour, fearing he might be gone, were they to defer the baptism until the morning. Their heroic christian faith was rewarded. Six miles the dear parents had come with their babe in a sleigh, through the piercing storm of frost and snow, that it might be born anew to Christ. At once the lights were relighted and the fires rekindled. A new joy pervaded the whole place. It was happy as a Christmas night. A babe was born again "of water and the Holy Ghost, and made heir with Christ to a Heavenly kingdom." The event, as of record in the parish baptismal register of Chillicothe, is as follows: "1861, January 23rd, I baptized Catharine, born Nov. 4, 1860, daughter of Edmond Shine and Prudence Eccleston, his wife; Sponsor, Paulina Newman. John Hogan." Paulina Newman, the sponsor, was the venerable lady of the household. Her daughter, Miss Newman was the bride of the disappointed wedding. After the baptism I retired for a short time to rest. Early in the morning, in the midst of a blinding snow-storm, that had fairly obliterated the roads, I set out on the homeward journey, the birds of the air—victims of cold and hunger—falling down and fluttering in death in the snow around me. It was some hours in the night when I arrived at Chillicothe.

ONE MORE JANUARY BLAST.

In accordance with appointments previously made, I set out in January, 1868, on an extended mission, in the Missouri counties bordering on Iowa; and I preferred to go on horseback, as the roads were too rough and broken, to travel in a buggy. On Monday morning, January 6th, I left Chillicothe, and rode that day forty miles to Bancroft, where I said Mass on Tuesday. After Mass I rode fifteen miles to Bethany, where I said Mass on Wednesday. On Wednesday after Mass, I rode eighteen miles to the neighborhood of Eagleville, where I said Mass on Thursday, and likewise on Friday and Saturday; making inquiries and search all the while, for any Catholics, known to be residing in that region of country. On Saturday I rode to Akron, where I was to spend Sunday, January 12th. My Sunday appointment at Akron brought crowds of people—Catholics who who had gathered from far and near along the borders of Missouri and Iowa, and non-Catholics who were curious to see the rare sight in those days—a priest in that part of the country. After supper Saturday night, I said the Rosary and the Night Prayers, as usual, with the family where I stopped, then taught catechism and gave catechetical instructions; and afterwards began hearing confessions of those living in the house or who had come there to attend their religious duties, it being customary with me to

observe this order of work on Saturday evenings, so
as to lessen the labors of Sunday morning. Again
on Sunday morning I heard confessions and gave
catechetical instructions, as I found people waiting
for one or the other duty. At eleven o'clock I celebrated Mass, at which I preached a sermon on the
Gospel, and gave Holy Communion to many who
had not been to the Holy Table for years. After
Mass I baptized some children, and likewise several
adults, the children of Catholics, whom I hastily prepared, as well as I could, for the reception of this
sacrament essential to salvation. Next, according
to previous appointment, I preached in the school
house, which was near by, to a large and attentive
assemblage of non-Catholics; who then, for the
first time in their lives, heard a word from a
priest on Catholic doctrine. When the sermon was
over, it was half past two o'clock, and my first opportunity for breakfast, which I rarely partook of on
Sundays, until my duties to my expectant congregations had been complied with. Having partaken of
the late afternoon breakfast, I hastily strapped fast
on my horse's back, the valise and leathern saddlebags, in which I carried vestments, books, and necessary clothing; and then mounting, I turned my
horse's head north-eastward, to go to Lineville—a
small town near the Iowa state line, and at a much
greater distance from Akron than I had imagined.
The weather was intensely cold, and the ground which

was covered with snow, was icy and rough. In a little while I crossed the Thompson Fork of Grand River on the ice, on a trail of straw laid across, to prevent cattle from slipping and falling down. Thence my course was East by North, with a freezing blast and small dry snow striking me fast in the face. It was useless that I tried to dodge the cold, by turning my head aside to right or left. I needed to keep a straight onward outlook, to guide my horse safe, over broken roads, ravines and tree stumps that beset my way. The night came on apace, and with it the discouraging thought, that I was still many miles from a certain saw-mill, at which, as had been previously arranged, a guide was to meet me at the hour of sunset. When I had reached the saw-mill, it was three hours past sunset, and no guide was there to lead me on, over roads of which I knew little. I learned afterwards from the guide, that he turned his horse's head homeward, when one hour had passed after my failure to arrive on time, at the appointed meeting place. It was his conviction, he said, that I was not on the road at all; and that I had been deterred by the bad weather from venturing out on the journey. There was no help for me. In the storm, I had to weather it out, as best I could. To add to my hardship and discouragement, I wandered much out of the right way, and during the whole time was uncertain whether I was in the right road or not. It was past midnight when I reached my destination—a certain farm house, three miles east of Lineville—within a stone's throw, on the Missouri side, of the inter-state line. Dismounting, I knocked on the door of the farm house, and soon the inmates, who were fast asleep, arose and came to my relief. I was so overcome by cold, drowsiness, and fatigue, that I was scarcely able to walk. My chest and lungs were aching. The nipping frosty breeze and impinging snow-flakes, in the teeth of which I had held my face constantly for eight consecutive hours, together with the predisposition to ailment of throat and lungs, brought on by several hours of preaching at Akron, had nearly done their fatal work on me. In the morning I had bleeding lungs, the first and only attack of the kind, in my life. I steadied myself however, firmly and quietly, to hear confessions, celebrate Mass, and administer a few baptisms; but without any attempt at preaching. These duties over, I felt myself quite unable to continue my appointments for places in the counties of Mercer and Putnam, where many Catholics had settled, as I was told, and were without a priest to attend to them. These I intended to visit as soon as I should be able. Having strapped my baggage on my horse's back, I set out for home; travelling at a slow gait by way of Ravenna, to the neighborhood of Princeton, where I stayed at the house of a Catholic settler over night, and celebrated Mass next morning. Thence I travelled

by way of Goshen and Modena to Edinburg, in
Grundy county. At Edinburg, I likewise stayed
with some Catholic settlers that I found there, saying
Mass for them and baptizing their children next
morning. From Edinburg, I proceeded towards
Chillicothe, where I arrived Wednesday evening,
the 15th of January, the third day of my journey
from Lineville. I was thankful to God for the
strength given me to reach home alive, if not in good
health. At Chillicothe, whilst resting to regain my
wasted strength and energy, I received a strange
document, written in Latin and in a peculiar hand,
which translated into English reads as follows.

CHAPTER XXII.

THE STRANGE DOCUMENT.

"RIGHT Reverend Sir: Among many things of advantage to the Catholic religion, that were done by the United States Plenary Council held in Baltimore in 1866, the proposition of the Most Reverend Fathers therein assembled, to erect new episcopal sees for the greater increase of the christian name and the more diligent care of the faithful, is clearly to be recorded. Since therefore one of these new sees is designated to be the city of St. Joseph, in the province of St. Louis, it has pleased our Most Holy Father, with the advice of the Sacred Congregation of the Propaganda, to entrust the government of it to Your Right Reverence, whose doctrine and virtue have been clearly vouched for by trustworthy recommendations. The Holy Father is therefore fully persuaded that you will use all your care and diligence, so that having become a perfect example to the flock, you will so bear the aforesaid episcopal burthen, as to gather and lay up a most abundant harvest in the store-house of Jesus Christ. Furthermore, the Apostolic Letters by which the aforesaid office will be given into your charge, as likewise, the necessary Apostolic Faculties therefor, will, by my care, be sent to you as soon as possible. Beseeching God to bestow upon you and your diocese His choicest blessings, I am yours most devotedly.

At Rome from the Sacred Congregation of the Propagation of the Faith; January 26, 1868;

H. CAPALTI,   ALEXANDER CARDINAL BARNABO,
    Secretary.   Prefect."

BEAUTIFUL SPRING TIME.

The threatened illness brought on by exposure and fatigue in the month of January having entirely passed away, I was soon out again, revisiting the missions of Bethany, Eagleville, Akron and Princeton, where, as before, I said Mass, heard confessions, gave instructions, administered baptism, and afforded opportunity to the faithful to comply fully with their christian duties. Later on in the spring, or rather in the month of May, towards the end of the Paschal Time, I set out to complete the missionary journey, which the inclement weather of January had compelled me to temporarily abandon. But how different now from stormy midwinter were the beautiful days of spring. Vegetation had already come on apace. The elder, hazel, elm, and the silver maple were in full vigor of life. The willow, gooseberry, and rose bushes had shaken off their icy fringes, and were bursting their petals into full leaf and blossom. The peach, apple and pear trees, gaily dressed in exuberant bloom, were scattering over the ground their superabundant floral wealth, that filled the air with sweetest fragrance. Everywhere the wild plum and cherry, and the red-bud and flowering locust, had spread out their bright many colored banners, and their drapery of magnificence and glory. Far and near and all around, and away in the remotest distances of the horizon, the endless prairie in its bright mantle of green, dotted with turretted islands of leafy forest, and traversed by winding streams fringed with waving willows and drooping elms, basked and glowed in the warm sunshine that gave all nature life. Where now were the piercing winds, the frozen icy bands, and the pelting snow flakes of winter? The ploughman, too, was abroad, with gladness in his steps, following his merry horses, as they rushed the ploughshare through the mellow lea. It was no wonder that the joyousness of his resonant voice, as he talked and sang to his team, outvied the little birds of the forest, that sang on the bushes and on the tree-tops around him; for in his gladsome heart, he foresaw the teeming granaries and the fruitful harvests, that were to reward his labors. O beautiful prairies of Missouri, so often and for so many years the joy of my heart, well I have said in my younger days, when first I heard of your transcendent loveliness, and when friends would tempt my youthful feet to other climes; O no, leave me my joy; Missouri is my home; I love her for her woods and prairies; amid these let my grave be made; under the bending boughs of her forests I long to die.

MISSION WORK CONTINUED.

I visited Milan, Clarksburg, and Unionville in the month of May. At Milan I preached in the Court House in the evening. The whole town flocked to the Palace of Justice to hear the priest. Mothers were there in great numbers, holding up their wondering babies in their arms. The dear little babies cried louder than I could talk. But how could I be so unfeeling as to tell the loving mothers of the dear little children to go out. Young and old, they were all welcome. I preached against noise for half an hour. Then, the little innocents having fallen fast asleep, I had the audience to myself, and great was the attention paid to me. I baptized many infants and adults at Milan and Clarksburg. And many at these places, as also at Unionville, went to Holy Communion. It was very edifying to see children of twelve and fourteen years of age, who though never before having seen a priest or been in a Catholic church, were nevertheless so thoroughly instructed in piety and christian doctrine by their worthy parents, as to be fully prepared on that first occasion, to receive not only baptism but likewise their First Communion. My journey homeward from Milan was a pleasant one. I travelled from Milan to Scottsville, ten miles; thence south over the beautiful prairie on the west side of Parson Creek, twenty miles to Collier's Mill; thence six miles to Chillicothe. It was a long ride on horseback for one day. But my horse was a willing, gentle animal. And as the journey was through a beautiful country, I enjoyed it very much. My horse, too, must have enjoyed the journey. Occasionally, as the fresh prairie grass seemed very tempting, I let him browse a little. He reached his stable in good condition and with unhalting gait.

CHURCH BUILDING AT CAMERON.

At this time I pushed on the work of building a church at Cameron, the site of which I had acquired in October, 1866, partly by donation and partly by purchase from the Hannibal and St. Joseph Railroad Company. The building was commenced in the spring and completed early in the summer of 1868. Cameron had at this time become a place of some importance, by its recent connection with Kansas City by railroad.

ROMAN DOCUMENTS.

The Bulls erecting the new see of St. Joseph and appointing its first bishop were issued at Rome March 3rd, 1868. Forwarded without delay, they had arrived, and were lying on my desk some time. I could not defer longer to examine them, and to conclude what to do. On unfolding the parchment, I found that the limits assigned to the new diocese were that part of the state of Missouri lying between the Missouri and Chariton rivers, which comprised about half the missionary district that I had been attending, with the older missions of Liberty, Weston, and St. Joseph attached thereto. That I was surprised at what had been done does not at all express what my feelings were. With the greatest respect for the Sacred Congregation of the Propaganda, I could not help seeing, that either it had acted on an important matter without the full information; or that it had placed too great faith in the progressiveness of a backward corner of the state of Missouri, to suppose that it could become even an insignificant diocese in a hundred years. In the allotment it seemed to have been borne in mind, that the mantle of apostolic poverty would be the very best inheritance for the bishop of St. Joseph; and that no opportunity should be given him, to unlearn the fair knowledge he had acquired, of the mode of living of the fathers of the desert. I thought it my duty to make thorough investigation as to what exactly comprised the new diocese of St. Joseph. What I found, was, that throughout its whole extent, there were not as many Catholics, as would, if all were together, make one congregation, such as could be easily attended by two priests. The statistics are as follows:

THE NEW DIOCESE.

CONGREGATIONS	FAMILIES	SOULS
Pro-Cathedral Parish	200	1000
Im. Conception, St. Joseph	50	250
Chillicothe and out missions	130	650
Liberty and out missions	50	250
Weston and out missions	90	450
Conception and Maryville	80	400
6	600	3000

THE PRO-CATHEDRAL.

The church edifices were of the poorest kind. The largest, the pro-cathedral, was a low, narrow, squalid brick house, built in three different sections, and at three different times. The floor was below the street level, and much of it quite underground. The walls and roof were held together by wooden stanchions bolted outside on the walls, and by hog-chains inside, athwart the little building. The site was in a hollow, in the curve of an open sewer or creek; the overflow from which, with every rain, poured mud and muck through the doors and chinky foundations in upon the floor of the rickety structure. Around the church was a dense growth of weeds, shrubs, and low intertangled shade trees;moss-covered from the constant wet of the overflow of the creek, as were likewise the walls of the building. There had been at one time a fence around the church, but it was now a jagged outline of rents and gaps; evidently made so by the assaults of droves of hogs that frequented the place, and that took great delight in ploughing up the soft mold with their long snouts, and rubbing their mucky backs and sides against the church walls, doors, and door posts. The hogs were in possession, and judging by their diligence, the palm was theirs for unequaled church-going qualities. With very subdued, if not altogether crushed feelings, I returned to Chillicothe, to meditate upon what further steps I should take. The several bishops appointed for their respective sees in the United States, on the same day that I was appointed to mine, had for the most part already received consecration. One was consecrated in May, four in July, four in August, one in the first days of September, one had absolutely declined consecration, and the remaining two (of whom I was one) were still hesitating what to do. Among those consecrated in July I was called upon to take my place, but I could not then consent to do so.

FINAL SURRENDER.

That the dignity and sacredness of the episcopal office is incomparably above human merit and worldly station, is what I would not gainsay, nor would I dare to ascribe purposes but the most exalted to the Holy See for the action it had taken in the hope of advancing religion. And if, doing away with pride and selfishness, I could also forget my unworthiness and sinfulness, in submitting to the fearful burthen and responsibility, made doubly so by its poverty and indigency, my motive would be, obedience to the will of God and to the Holy See, and dependence upon God for the necessary divine help. Also, I could not help thinking, that when eleven years before, I undertook, against all hope of success, the apparently very foolish task of opening missions in North Missouri, where all the odds were against me, it was because of my confidence in the protection and intercession of the Mother of my Redeemer, the feast of whose Nativity, so portentive of joy and blessing to the world, the Church was then celebrating. That same joyful, hope-inspiring feast was now again at hand. My devotion, too, to St. Joseph was propitious. Early in life I had added his blessed provident name, to my baptismal one, at Confirmation. I had a refuge in him, therefore, as my protector and patron with God, and in his humble patience and uncomplaining poverty, I had a consolation and a model. With the Flight into Egypt, for coat of arms, graven on my episcopal seal, I could, though with tears, break the ties that bound me to my beloved mission home—the Nazareth of my earlier years. I received consecration in St. Louis on the Feast of the Holy Name of Mary, Sunday, September the 13th, 1868. The following Sunday, devoted to the contemplation of the Sorrows of the Mother of God at the foot of the Cross, I was on duty at the pro-cathedral in St. Joseph.

—FINIS—

INDEX.
CHAPTER I.

	PAGE
Missionary Opportunity	1
Outward bound	1
Mounted	2
Predicting	3
Mulhollandists and Murphyites	3
Camp Garryowen	4
Packet Spread-Eagle	5
Slavery in Missouri	6
Slavery's better side	7
Hibernians and Jaegers	9
Homeward bound	11
The north-west passage	12

CHAPTER II.

A duty sanctioned	13
Friendship's pleading	13
Humors of Center Point	14
A telling sermon	14
Social enjoyment	15
John the Baptist	17
Chillicothe	18
A congregation of one	19
The priest in town	20

CHAPTER III.

Milan and the Milanese	22

True Nobility	23
An after-supper colloquy	25
The Universalists; what do you think of them?	27
The old Priest; what do you think of him?	28
Retiring to rest	30
Departing in wonder	30

CHAPTER IV.

Irish Brown	32
John the Baptist again	33
The hamlet of Mirabile	34
Discouragement	35

CHAPTER V.

Main purpose not advanced	37
Abnormal	37
The remedy	39
Surveying	39
My dear friend Father Fox	40

CHAPTER VI.

The shanty in the rosin-weeds	42
Dying in a cold cabin	43
Born in a stable	44

CHAPTER VII.

Father Walsh the emigrant's friend	47
The information gathered	49
Land offices and land surveying	50

CHAPTER VIII.

Church building at Chillicothe	54
Chillicothe and the fine arts	55
You know not the day nor the hour	56

CHAPTER IX.

Called southward 58
A difficulty 59
The new settlement 59
Society in Southern Missouri 60
Getting acquainted 62
Rev. Tim Reeves 63
Another Reverend 65
A sick call 66
The divine protection 66
Pulpit and penitentiary 68

CHAPTER X.

Old friends crying for help . 69
A new difficulty 70
The difficulty removed 71
Southward once more 71
Again northward and out of season 72

CHAPTER XI.

Travelling 73
Water-logged 74
The rescue 75
Rocks and shoals 76
Weathering a gale 77
The wildness of youth 78
God's unsearchable ways 79

CHAPTER XII.

White for the harvest 80
Missionary Time Table 82
Railroad and telegraph free 83

Ascension Thursday, 1860 84
Temples of the Living God 85
Bancroft 86
Bethany 87
Eagleville 87
Hickory Branch 87
Brookfield 88
Macon City 90
The savage Russians 90
Macon City again 93

CHAPTER XIII.

War's alarms 94
War's devastations 95
The rugged issue 96
Standing by the South 97
Holding to the Union 99
Mobilizing for battle 99
The deathly chasm 101
The Church militant 102
One hundred miles of fire 106

CHAPTER XIV.

Straightening the twigs 109
My gentle lambs 111
The roll-call 112

CHAPTER XV.

Bushwhackers and guerillas 116
A perilous night 116
Sunday's blessed dawn 119
Oh, the horrid crime 120

CHAPTER XVI.

Bogus Americans 123
Testing our mettle 124
Indictment 125
Catch him first 127
A man's enemies his own household 128
"Drury, dear, how are you?" 129
"List, list, O list" (Hamlet) 130

CHAPTER XVI.

The ring of true metal 133
The Brookfield meeting 134
Reply to the Brookfield delegation 137
On the altar of his country 141
Before the judgment seat 143
Persecuted in one city, flee into another 145
In the Adair Circuit Court 147

CHAPTER XVIII.

The Cummings case 149
Honorable Reverdy Johnson 149
Reply to Brookfield delegation quoted 150
United States Supreme Court decision 151

CHAPTER XIX.

"In nothing be ye terrified" Philip. 1:28 153
Where God is denied there the devil has power 155
"Bring in the priests of the Church." 156
Afflictions and consolations 159
Consolations and afflictions 160
The haunted house 162
Beelzebub cast out 165

From and ill end deliver him, O Lord ... 167
CHAPTER XX.
St. Bridget's church, Peabody ... 170
Greater than a Centurion. ... 171
Episcopal visitation ... 173
Confirmed at Brookfield ... 173
Confirmed at Chillicothe ... 174
"For better, for worse" ... 185
Seek not your future to know ... 177
CHAPTER XXI.
Climate ... 181
Indian Summer ... 181
Seemingly beautiful ... 182
Deceived again ... 183
Again deceived and turned robber ... 183
Blustering mid-winter ... 185
The disappointed wedding ... 186
You must be born again ... 190
One more January blast ... 192
CHAPTER XXII.
The strange document ... 197
Beautiful spring-time ... 198
Mission work continued ... 200
Roman documents ... 201
Church building at Cameron ... 201
The new diocese ... 203
The pro-cathedral ... 203
Submission ... 204